John Berger

D0771647

Titles in the series Critical Lives present the work of leading cultural figures of the modern period. Each book explores the life of the artist, writer, philosopher or architect in question and relates it to their major works.

In the same series

Georges Bataille
Stuart Kendall

Fyodor Dostoevsky
Robert Bird

Edweard Muybridge
Marta Braun

Charles Baudelaire
Rosemary Lloyd

Marcel Duchamp
Caroline Cros

Vladimir Nabokov
Barbara Wyllie

Simone de Beauvoir
Ursula Tidd

Sergei Eisenstein
Mike O'Mahony

Pablo Neruda
Dominic Moran

Samuel Beckett
Andrew Gibson

Michel Foucault
David Macey

Octavio Paz
Nick Caistor

Walter Benjamin
Esther Leslie

Mahatma Gandhi
Douglas Allen

Pablo Picasso
Mary Ann Caws

Jorge Luis Borges
Jason Wilson

Jean Genet
Stephen Barber

Edgar Allan Poe
Kevin J. Hayes

Constantin Brancusi
Sanda Miller

Derek Jarman
Michael Charlesworth

Ezra Pound
Alec Marsh

William S. Burroughs
Phil Baker

Alfred Jarry
Jill Fell

Jean-Paul Sartre
Andrew Leak

Coco Chanel
Linda Simon

James Joyce
Andrew Gibson

Erik Satie
Mary E. Davis

Noam Chomsky
Wolfgang B. Sperlich

Franz Kafka
Sander L. Gilman

Gertrude Stein
Lucy Daniel

Jean Cocteau
James S. Williams

Lenin
Lars T. Lih

Simone Weil
Palle Yourgrau

Salvador Dalí
Mary Ann Caws

Stéphane Mallarmé
Roger Pearson

Ludwig Wittgenstein
Edward Kanterian

Guy Debord
Andy Merrifield

Gabriel García Márquez
Stephen M. Hart

Frank Lloyd Wright
Robert McCarter

Claude Debussy
David J. Code

Karl Marx
Paul Thomas

John Berger

Andy Merrifield

REAKTION BOOKS

For John

Published by Reaktion Books Ltd
33 Great Sutton Street
London EC1V 0DX, UK

www.reaktionbooks.co.uk

First published 2012

Printed and bound in Great Britain
by Bell & Bain, Glasgow

British Library Cataloguing in Publication Data
Merrifield, Andy.
    John Berger. – (Critical lives)
    1. Berger, John.
    2. Authors, English – 20th century – Biography.
    3. Art critics – Great Britain – Biography.
    I. Title   II. Series
    828.9'1409-dc23

ISBN 978 1 86189 904 0

Contents

In *Play Me Something*.

Introduction: The Blackbird, the Badger and the King

Dressed in full-length leathers, riding his giant Honda Blackbird 1100 cc motorbike, John Berger cuts a curious figure for one of Europe's greatest living intellectuals. Residents of Quincy, the sleepy Savoyard village he's called home since 1975, are used to seeing this expat octogenarian (born Hackney, north London, 1926), this *costaud* white-haired novelist-playwright, film scriptwriter-poet, art critic-essayist, organic intellectual *engagé*, dart through windy Alpine passes at breakneck speeds, looking like a cross between a portly Batman and a real-life Jean Ferrero, Berger's alter ego from *To the Wedding*.

When Berger first moved to his Haute-Savoie beat, home was several modest rooms near Mieussy's Baroque church, with its striking bulbous spire. Summers then were passed on the *alpage* at Roche-Pallud, high up around 1,500 metres, in a chalet that had neither electricity nor running water. Descending into the vallée du Giffre, Berger later settled at a more clement 700 metres in a spacious old farmhouse, replete with barn and ornate spruce balcony, that had been empty for twenty years before his occupation. The property was constructed long before skiers and tourists and kitsch wooden holiday cabins colonized the area. Once upon a time, in a traditional abode like this, denizens ate and slept next to their beasts.

Berger had come to the Haute-Savoie from Geneva, some 50 kilometres due west, where he had lived since 1962, after cold-shouldering what he said was a closeted, provincial London in those days. So he uprooted himself, initially to an apartment next door to Geneva airport, at avenue de Mategnin, seemingly ready for a fast getaway, only to extricate himself again a decade or so later, dramatically in spite of the short distance, bedding himself down in the hay and in the land of semi-literate mountain peasants.

In coming to alpine France what had Berger forsaken? Phoniness, comfy literary cliques, the limelight, seductive city lights? Perhaps. What had he sought? Authenticity, the need to see and feel oppression close up, in its concrete form? Probably. What had he become? An immigrant? No, he had come here by choice, as a free man, as a privileged man – not as a seventh man. Besides, Berger's migration was against the migratory flow of the impoverished masses, those who move exclusively from the countryside to the city and not the other the other way around, not in a direction that corroborates privilege. That is presumably why he prefers to call himself a *stranger*, somehow always a stranger, even after 35 years of belonging, a stranger in a disappearing culture.

Perhaps Berger was trying to avoid what Guy Debord called 'the society of the spectacle', the topsy-turvy world in which falsity becomes an ultimate truth we are now compelled to respect, even worship. Debord quit Paris not long after Berger had quit London; the former had gone to the most lost of lost Auvergne villages, to a cottage, he said, 'that opened directly onto the Milky Way'. But Debord had come to cut himself off, to turn his back on society, playing no part in local auvergnate life. He lived behind a high stone wall, a wall a mason had built even higher at Debord's behest. Berger's house, by contrast, has no walls and is completely open to the street. Berger hates walls, walls of separation, walls that cut people off from one another, walls that keep people in as well as out. Anybody can come and knock at Berger's front door; his is one of the first houses on the left as you enter Quincy, just as the lane bends and narrows.

Even now, every year, the white-haired writer picks up a scythe and lends a hand with the summer haymaking, paying in kind for the farmhouse he continues to rent off old neighbours Dédé and his wife. Meanwhile, not only does Berger write about ordinary people; unlike most intellectuals he lives next door to a few, too, and has them around for dinner from time to time. (Writer Geoff Dyer, a Berger disciple, recalls dining at the Bergers' sandwiched between a Mieussy plumber and photographer Henri Cartier-Bresson.[1]) Rather than turning his back on locals, Berger has embraced them, has integrated himself within village life with his American wife, Beverly, even raising a kid there – Yves, an artist, born in 1976, who attended the local school and now lives next door; he uses papa's barn as his studio. (Berger also has a daughter, Katya, a translator and film critic, and Jacob, a filmmaker, both from an earlier, formative relationship with the Russian-born linguist Anya ('Anna') Bostock, with whom Berger penned several essays and translated the poetic works of Aimé Césaire and Bertolt Brecht. G., Berger's Booker Prize-winning novel, is dedicated to Anya, and to 'her sisters in Women's Liberation'.)

Berger claims he came to the Haute-Savoie to learn, to understand an endangered species, to see and feel oppression first-hand, mimicking with the French peasantry what Karl Marx's old comrade Frederick Engels did with Manchester's working class, understanding their 'condition', their worsening condition. Berger wanted to see where Europe's migrant workers set off from, wanted to witness the old life they had left behind. 'I came to listen', he says, 'in order to write, not to speak on their behalf. I wanted to touch something that had a relevance way beyond the French Alps. Far from retreating, I was homing in on a point that touched a nerve bud about a very important development in contemporary world history.'

Chez Berger there is still no inside wc, and every May – after the snow has gone and before the summer flies swarm – the writer

Haymaking in the 1970s.

Haymaking in the 1980s.

exchanges pen for spade and pushes his wheelbarrow across the
backyard to clear out a year's worth of shit – his own, his family's
and his guests'. He has consecrated the act in a suitably pungent,
scatological essay, 'A Load of Shit', pointedly autobiographical,
laying into 'elite intellectuals' like Milan Kundera because they
don't like getting crap on their hands, because they look down
on muck and on those who shovel it. 'In the world of modern
hygiene', Berger says, 'purity has become a purely metaphysical
or moralistic term. It has lost all sensuous reality.'[2]

It would be wonderful to be a fly on the wall somewhere nearby,
watching Berger at his outhouse shovelling shit. And to meet Mick,
the neighbour's mischievous dog, who mauls sheep and comes
to lend Berger a paw. 'The shit slides out of the barrow when it's
upended', he says, 'with a slurping dead weight. And the foul sweet
stench goads, nags teleologically.' The smell is of decay, to be sure,
like pig excrement, because like pigs humans are carnivores and
our appetites are indiscriminate; but it's not a smell of shame or
sin as puritans would insist: decaying shit should have nothing to

do with a loathing of the body. 'Its colours are burnished gold, dark brown, black: colours of Rembrandt's painting of Alexander the Great in his helmet.'

You have to hand it to Berger, invoking Rembrandt, bringing art criticism down to earth, waxing poetic about putrefaction. And that little parable about the rosy apple falling into cow dung, a story from the village school son Yves recounts to his papa: 'Good morning, Madame la Pomme', the cowpat says, 'how are you feeling?' No response from la pomme: such a conversation is below the apple's dignity. 'It's fine weather, isn't it? Madame la Pomme?' Again silence. A few minutes later somebody walks by, picks up the apple and bites into it. 'See you in a little while, Madame la Pomme!' says the cow shit, irrepressibly.

It's not that Berger likes shovelling shit. It seems that confronting shit, knowing what it is, where it comes from, how it smells, keeps him in contact with his nose and his body, with sensuous reality. And sensuous reality seems to be what Berger yearns for: the need for authentic experience, for a life without rubber gloves, unmediated by mod cons and gadget commodities, by air conditioning and central heating. Berger's body seems to want to *feel* and *smell* just as his brain wants to think. Perhaps Berger sought, still seeks, wants us to seek, the rawness of experience Spanish poet Federico García Lorca called 'deep song', something 'imbued with the mysterious colour of primordial ages', akin 'to the trilling of birds, the crowing of the rooster, the natural music of forest and fountain'.

Maybe Berger himself is searching for a deep sense of place, for a sense of belonging, for a *foyer* in a vast world, a world that's increasingly getting flattened and compartmentalized by neoliberal capitalism. A foyer, he says, in a barely disguised biographical essay, '*L'Exil*' (appearing in French), incarnates 'the centre of the world' – not a geographical centre but an *existential* centre; a foyer establishes itself like a Leibnizian monad, like a 'mirror of the

Intellectual with wheelbarrow.

universe', like a part that somehow internalizes all parts, like a partial totality. Quincy, for Berger, is a sort of existential homeland, 'the heart of the real' in a world that's becoming ever more global and *ir*real, ever more 'extra-territorial'. 'Without a foyer, without a centre to your world, there's nowhere to take refuge: you're lost in non-Being and *ir*reality. Without a foyer, everything, including your own self, decomposes into fragments.' That's why, Berger says, all artists who achieve universality are closely bound with the local and the particular, like Cézanne and his beloved Provençal mountain, like Jack Yeats and his wild west coast of Ireland.

People who read Berger, who love him and his words, are often searching for the like themselves, searching for a deeper, richer meaning to the world, to their world. That's why his stripped-down prose, his increasingly mystical words, carefully chosen earthly (and earthy) words, always strike a chord, always grab you by the collar, force you to join in. Berger's take on art is similarly compelling. He sees paintings not so much as canvases hung on smart gallery walls than as keys to the meaning of life, windows of our world, images of human sensuality and destiny. Berger empathizes with artists and their subjects, gets inside their heads and bodies, and has written jubilantly, inimitably, about Picasso, Léger, Van Gogh, Gauguin, Modigliani, Courbet, Matisse, Caravaggio, Goya, Velázquez and many more. (Jackson Pollock's paintings, he once said, 'are like pictures painted on the inside of his mind'.)

If we stare at paintings, Berger says, paintings begin to stare back at us, tell us stories about ourselves: 'The gaze of Aesop makes me hesitate', he notes in front of Velázquez's great canvas.

> He's intimidating, he has a kind of arrogance. A pause for
> thought. No, he's not arrogant. But he doesn't suffer fools
> gladly. The presence of Aesop refers to nothing except what

he has felt and seen. Refers to no possessions, to no institutions, to no authority or protection. If you weep on his shoulder, you'll weep on the shoulder of his life. If you caress his body, it will recall the tenderness it knew in childhood.[3]

In 'Ways of Seeing' (1972), the polemical BBC TV series, Berger helped reinvent art criticism. 'Ways of Seeing' popularized art, democratized it in both its form and content. Berger helped deepen one's appreciation of art, of the pleasure of looking at art, sharpening one's critical eye around artistic production: he brought conceptual gifts to the BBC production team's visual gifts. Words blended with images to become dramatic television, brilliantly putting art in its rightful class and gender context, transforming artwork from unique connoisseurial worship, showing how art is a reproducible commodity, a celebration of private appropriation, a piece of commerce, a medium for advertising, something open to the public. Henceforth art and aesthetics was no longer an exclusive mandarin preoccupation; Gainsborough's *Mr and Mrs Andrews* would never look the same again ('PRIVATE PROPERTY, TRESPASSERS KEEP OUT!'). Berger taught generations of people to challenge art, and to demystify classic paintings; *Ways of Seeing*, the spin-off book, has never been out of print since.

In texts like *Another Way of Telling* (1982), full of Berger's long - standing Swiss collaborator Jean Mohr's vivid black and white photos, Berger also coined a new, utterly original way of telling stories, of portraying lives, of sketching landscapes and vistas with simple words set alongside direct, almost artless images. What emerged was a very striking poetic humanism, speaking out over distances and across cultures; it was pretty much as Wordsworth had put it in the preface of *Lyrical Ballads*: here were men speaking to men.

In *Another Way of Telling* lots of images linger. One is of an old peasant shepherd, Marcel, who, with his 50 cows, laboured high on the *alpage* around Sommand. Weatherbeaten and wizened, the diminutive Marcel is out in the open air, out with his dogs and little grandson, out with his cattle. Two other photos pair off a close-up of Marcel's gentle eyes and wrinkled face with a cow's gentle eyes and wrinkled face; the similarity is uncanny.

Elsewhere Marcel is sitting on a stool in front of a table adorned with a chequered tablecloth. His little wooden shack is primitive yet dignified. Pots dangle over the sink; Marcel's kitchen is fully equipped! He's eating something – a morsel of bread perhaps, or maybe a croissant – dunking it into a bowl of coffee. It's obvious he's poor, but it's equally clear that Marcel knows some tricks about the good life, about food and drink, about taste and ordinary everyday joys: a piece of bread, a cup of black coffee, drunk out of a little bowl. Pictures like this, and the accompanying text, let us dream of Alpine summits and snow-capped peace, and offer us an ideal of the good life on the sly. Berger and Mohr take us there, help us pose our own questions about place and belonging, about deep experience and feeling connected to things.

Collaborating with Jean Mohr.

Berger has called himself a 'jack of all trades', and it's that which makes his work so important and approachable, so worth reading and considering. All his life he has maintained his independence from institutions, voiced intellectual ambitions that went and still go against the grain of received ideas, those that hold to specialization, to a narrowing of vistas rather than an opening up of horizons. At the same time there is a tremendous depth of feeling in his novels and short stories, in his essays and poems, that stir something inside us, savant and layperson alike, making his writings 'popular' in a way many intellectual works are not. Berger strays beyond the obligatory disciplinary border controls and divisions of mental labour, all of which provides him with a richness of insight yet creates havoc for any study of his life and work: how to put together the person, the life, the times, as well as the intellectual contributions without hacking apart this delicate totality, this range and diversity; how to do it without severing its inextricable unity and finely tuned harmony?

Berger cites Gauguin to explain his reluctance to write explicit autobiography: everything about the artist, Gauguin said, can be found in his art, in his brushstrokes, should we have the nerve to get close enough, to really look, to get beyond *copying distance*. Thus in dealing with Berger's art, in analysing and criticizing it, in admiring and edging nearer and nearer to it, we will somehow discover, unveil, the man himself, and his times, our times. That's what Berger seems to tell us, rather like the way Caravaggio sneaks about his own paintings, sometimes haunting the background, other times losing his head completely.

Berger says that writing should be an act of joining together different aspects of reality, of making sense of ostensibly disparate things, of demystifying their productive and creative process. This book will try to do exactly that with Berger's own oeuvre. It will move thematically rather than strictly chronologically, try to give meaning to Berger's own experience, to his art and his politics, attempt to be as multifaceted and as freewheeling as the subject-matter itself. It will necessitate a good deal of to-ing and fro-ing, shifting retrospectively as well as prospectively, fleshing things out inductively as well as deductively. For Berger the critic, concern is foremost with analysis and interpretation, with facts, with *revealing* truth. For Berger the artist, concern is above all with creation, with feeling and imagination, with *creating* truth. Berger's best work constantly moves between the two realms, blurs the boundaries between fact and fiction, manoeuvring between each, much as Pierre and Paul in Alain Tanner's *La Salamandre*, the journalists investigating the case of would-be murderer Rosemonde, incarnate objective and subjective forms of knowledge respectively.

The present book will attempt to enter Berger's world, enter between the lines, between his black and white spaces, enter into his imagination, stitching together texts, politics and life into a (hopefully) coherent whole, revealing some truths here while speculating on others there, all the while encountering his many friends and influences – Spinoza, Marx, Ernst Fischer, Frederick Antal, George Orwell, Walter Benjamin, Georg Lukács, Simone Weil, Nazim Hikmet, James Joyce. Along the way, we will rendez-vous in real and imagined places, and meet assorted characters, highbrow and lowbrow, human and animal, the living as well as the dead. Especially the dead. Storytellers, Berger once claimed, borrow their authority from the dead – they're 'Death's secretaries' – it's death that hands storytellers like Berger the file, and the 'file is full of sheets of uniformly black paper'. Raconteurs, he says in 'The Secretary of Death' (see *The White Bird*), must 'have eyes for reading them and from this file they construct a story for the living'. 'All the storyteller needs or has is the capacity to read what is written in black.'[4]

Perhaps decades of riding a motorbike at high speeds on mountain passes has taught Berger the thin line between living ecstasy and rapid death: a split-second lapse, a patch of black ice, a mishap by somebody else, a careless motorist, a drunk . . . it's all over, you are over the edge, rolling down, down into the valley of the damned. Or maybe living next to peasants has sensitized Berger's awareness of death, the proximity of a dying people, to moribund traditions desperately trying to cling on to grim life. Whatever the case, knowing about death somehow lets storytellers like Berger marvel at the wonders of the life spirit, of daily life as epic drama and Greek tragedy, as if flying into the light of the dark black night. Sometimes, he admits in *Photocopies*, 'it seems that, like an ancient Greek, I write mostly about the dead and death. If this is so, I can only add that it is done with a sense of urgency which belongs uniquely to life.'

The artist, Berger says, has a deep moral obligation. For that reason, any Berger monograph also has to explore his moral visions of a democratic world, understand his support for the Zapatistas, recognize how an Alpine peace has whetted his appetite for transnational confrontation. He has exiled himself only to engage militantly with the world, to feel and negotiate what Simone Weil called the 'gravity and grace' of human existence. Here, too, we must keep a firm grip on Berger's longstanding Marxist credentials, which condemn the brutality that often accompanies everyday experience and sensuality. Berger labels himself 'amongst other things' a Marxist, and his critical edge is always sharper when it's subtly tender rather than blatantly angry. He is at his most effective when that tenderness communicates moral outrage. Berger's worst writing, like the worst Marxism, is when moral outrage becomes precious, when it becomes obvious or contrived, when moral indignation *leads* artistic flourish.

In what follows, we'll hitch a ride on Berger's motorbike, holding on tight, maybe even for dear life, trusting this road goer to take us to a destination, somewhere probably not terribly far away. We'll trust him to let us experience a sense of travelling. We'll hopefully arrive somewhere, too. We'll make a few stop-offs, perhaps places you know already, perhaps not. Friends and neighbours of Berger will tell you that if the caped crusader's at home, his giant Honda Blackbird motorbike will be there, stationary, off the road, parked in front of his rustic chalet. In the golden Alpine sunshine its raw power will glisten serene, almost Zen-like. But the tranquillity can be deceptive: anybody who sees it will also sense that this is a bike always ready for *action*, always ready for radical *mobilization*.

'Everything's a question of how you lean', explains bike man Jean Ferrero to his daughter Ninon in *To the Wedding*, Berger's thinly disguised fictional cross-frontier *dérive*. It is Ninon who recounts the lesson as Papa journeys to her wedding, to a little village in Italy on the Po delta, Ninon the daughter who has just been diagnosed as HIV positive.[5] A little parable for life: it's all a matter of how you lean, how you deal with inertia, how you deal with the laws of life's gravity as well as life's grace.

> If anything on wheels wants to corner or change direction, a centrifugal force comes into play. This force tries to pull us out of the bend into the straight, according to a law called the Law of Inertia, which always wants energy to save itself. In a corner situation it's the straight that demands least energy and so our fight starts. By tipping our weight over into the bend, we shift the bike's centre of gravity and this counteracts the centrifugal force and the Law of Inertia!

It's quite a motorbike that Jean and John ride. Even Honda suggests that its Blackbird 1100 has a ridiculous top speed: 275 km/h (170.8 mph). It's a pricey aficionado's machine, aesthetically beautiful yet lethal in the hands of a rookie. Berger has ridden a motorbike almost all his adult life. He knows about bikes and has not lost his nerve. His bike has an acceleration that blows your mind: 0–100 km/h in 2.4 seconds and 0–200 km/h in 8.7 seconds!

En moto, Quincy.

You'll make it on time to any wedding on that thing. Yet 'the speed of motorbikes (and speed has everything to do with mass and weight)', Berger says, 'is often thought of as brutal (and it can be), but it can also whisper of an extraordinary tenderness.'

Blackbirds are solitary creatures by nature, preferring woodland and heaths as habitats, greenery near open ground. They have a fine lyrical repertoire and sing richly and clearly with a mellow voice, like the dulcet tones of a flute. And although black has connotations of death and darkness, of mystery and evil, Berger sees it as the colour of sex, of black truffles, of making out in the bare earth under an oak tree. Just as John visualizes Jean in *To the Wedding*, we need to visualize Berger in his own kitchen, not far from an oak tree, anointing his sexy black Blackbird with pleasure and tenderness. We need to see him lovingly checking the brake fluid, the cooling liquid, the oil, the tyre pressure, gripping the chain with his left forefinger to test whether it's tight enough. Turning on the ignition, he watches the dials light up red and then he will examine the two headlights and hear the purr of his flute. Methodical gestures: careful and gentle, done as if the bike is a living organism, done at night in the kitchen in front of the stove.

In front of the stove, in the kitchen, is the warmest spot of Berger's farmhouse in winter. It's a cozy corner all visitors remember. (Berger says he feels comfortable in only two interior spaces: kitchens and artists' studios.) Apparently Berger's house is pretty beat-up inside. He likes it like that. All sorts of bike parts and gear will likely be spread about everywhere, amid stacks of books, loose papers, scythes and work boots, artists' crayons and pens. A while ago, a surprisingly affectionate article, 'Portrait of the Artist as a Wild Old Man', in *The Daily Telegraph* (23 July 2001), spoke about Berger's 'bashed-up home' and his curious affinity with the American polemicist Andrea Dworkin. 'She emerges as an intolerant castrating feminist', says Berger, 'but in her fiction you can see that she is incredibly open, sensuous and tender. There's a strange relationship between fury and devastating tenderness.'

Just like a motorbike, just like Berger himself: pissed-off and furious with the state of the world, with the free market Dark Age we now endure, yet full of devastating tenderness, too. In one of his essays in *The Shape of a Pocket*, Berger cites Dworkin saying: 'I have no patience with the untorn, anyone who hasn't weathered rough weather, fallen apart, been ripped to pieces, put herself back together, big stitches, jagged cuts, nothing nice. Then something shines out. But the ones all shined up on the outside, the ass wigglers, I'll be honest, I don't like them. Not at all.'

This is Berger's world, a world at once torn up and delicately calibrated. Not an ass wiggler in sight. He is an intense creator, a spontaneous sketcher and poet, a stream-of-consciousness writer, a man who invents a ripped-up world and puts it all back together, shining on the inside, feeling reality like the irrationalist Rousseau. And yet, curiously, he is also a meticulous rider and realist, evaluating how things function mechanically, probing objects critically and scientifically like the rationalist Descartes.

'Writing a poem is the opposite of riding a motorbike', Berger puts it himself in *Pages of the Wound*.

Riding, you negotiate at high speed around every fact you meet. Body and machine follow your eyes that find their way through, untouched. Your sense of freedom comes from the fact that the wait between decision and consequence is minimal . . . Poems are helpless before the facts. Helpless but not without endurance, for everything resists them. They find names for consequences, not for decisions. Writing a poem you listen to everything save what is happening now . . . On a bike the rider weaves through, and poems head in the opposite direction. Yet shared sometimes between the two, as they pass, there is the same pity of it.

Two different modes of experiencing the world, each thought to be opposed to one another – rational mechanics and aesthetic intuition – find an overleap in Berger's brain and in Berger's body, a common sharing, a reconciliation. They are unified as Berger meanders in a low gear up a lonely mountain pass, and as he scribbles on a blank white page . . .

One sunny April afternoon circa 2006, a quarter of a century after *Another Way of Telling* had first introduced the unassuming peasant Marcel Nicoud, Berger journeys once again up the *alpage* around Roche-Pallud – to Marcel's kingdom. Marcel was the king of this land, a land dominated by the 2,000-metre Pointe de Marcelly, crowned by a giant cross on a narrow sliver of rock which towers over Berger country – Mieussy, Taninges, Cluses and la vallée du Giffre. At these heights paragliders hover in cool mountain air; not far below, camouflaged in the rocks, marmots lie belly-down. Up here snow is not uncommon in June. And over yonder Mont Blanc, Europe's tallest mountain (4,800 metres), looms dreamily. The great White Mountain is not called that for nothing: forever snow-covered, in fine weather it looks luminously majestic, like candyfloss, radiant above other jagged peaks. In late afternoon, just before sunset, it becomes awesomely beautiful, a throbbing red-golden pulse absorbing the sun's final energy of the day. At dusk it shimmers with a bluely grey hue, seemingly about to recede into a slumbering calm. Even in pitch-black darkness you sense Mont Blanc's great hulking mass is lurking somewhere out there, in deep infinite space.

Marcel has been dead for seven years. His 50 cows, two dogs and handful of goats are long gone. But the chalet in which he ate, slept and dunked his bread is still there, more weatherbeaten than ever, more derelict, yet upright nonetheless. It's here, says Berger, where they tippled *gnôle* together, *eau de vie* – 50 per cent proof – and toasted each other's health. The two-room shack is no bigger than a small van. Some faded photos remain, pinned to the wooden planks that act as walls. The wooden table is still standing, around which Marcel and Berger 'exchanged stories, perhaps only fables; but like the way great fishermen's fables attempt to fathom an inexplicable ocean, our fables', says Berger, 'were attempts to figure out what we might consider as our original mystery: procreation'.[6]

In the bedroom is Marcel's single bed. He slept there in the same clothes he wore during the day. 'I touch the mattress', Berger says. 'I don't cry: he'd have found that undignified. I sense he's not far away.' Perhaps, in another life, Berger might have been Marcel (remember, *berger* is the French word for shepherd). Maybe Marcel is the alter ego John *le berger* never quite abandoned, never quite renounced, never could renounce, even as he operates in elite intellectual circles, even as he tries to affirm himself as a global citizen.

Suddenly, from a pile of hay, stacked up in corner of the king's shack, a badger emerges from its winter hibernation, sensing somebody close by, sensing danger. He marches out indignantly. He walks like a bear, and, turning his head occasionally, grunts and groans, hastening his discreet exit. Once outside, he stops, the white stripe on his fur rolled up like a sleeve of a shirt, unkempt, alert, crafty teller of stories. Yes, he walks like a bear, body stooped with age, unkempt, meticulous, alert, his white hair glowing in the sunlight – crafty teller of stories.

Over many years this crafty teller of stories has stashed away in his old barn boxes and boxes of rough, handwritten drafts of his novels, essays, short stories; loose clippings, photocopied letters and assorted paraphernalia of the creative process, of the hidden edifice of artistic production. In the summer of 2009 our story - teller brought these 80 dusty box files out of hibernation, donating almost everything to London's British Library, a lifetime of papers in a bumper harvest for Britain, as well as an amazing resource for rummaging researchers everywhere, preserved in perpetuity. To give them away, to *freely* give them away, Berger said, was a kind of relief. A weight was lifted. Besides, how could he put a monetary value on a relentless affair of the heart, on things that concern passion, imagination? When market forces seemingly dominate everyone and everything, this was a storyteller's potlatch, the badger's radical gift, a different concept of value that is non-negotiable, that is deeply *un*mercantile . . .

1

Seeing Eye

'Art is necessary in order that humans should be able to recognize and change the world. But art is also necessary by virtue of the magic inherent in it.'

Ernst Fisher, *The Necessity of Art*

'The greater the decrease in the social significance of an art form, the sharper the distinction between criticism and enjoyment by the public.'

Walter Benjamin, 'The Work of Art in the Age of Mechanical Reproduction'

Concentrate hard on a picture. Bring everything you have hitherto known and felt and learned to bear on this image. And then, when thought approaches the condition of physical labour, look harder still. Afterwards, with absolute clarity, and as simply as possible, begin to articulate what you see. 'That, in essence', says Geoff Dyer, 'is Berger's method.'[1]

Try doing it with someone like Van Gogh. 'His paintings', says Berger in the aptly named essay 'The Production of the World',

imitate the active existence – the labour of being – of what they depict. Take a chair, a bed, a pair of boots. His act of painting them was far nearer than that of any other painter to the carpenter's or the shoemaker's act of making them. He brings together the elements of the product – legs, cross bars, back, seat; sole, upper tongue, heel as though he too were fitting them together, *joining* them, and as if *being joined* constituted their reality.

Van Gogh was driven, obsessed, compelled to get closer and closer to the reality he had produce and reproduce, to the reality he would invent and make us believe. 'He takes us as close as any man can', Berger says, 'while remaining intact, to that permanent process by which reality is being produced.'[2]

What we see is itself an act of production: the seeing eye is never innocent, never objective in its vision, never without motive in the act of looking. In looking at Van Gogh, in looking at any painting, in looking at the world itself, what we see is conditioned by who we are, where we've been and what we've seen before. We bring to our gaze habits and conventions; looking belies those conventions, looking belies our class, looking belies sometimes what we must *un*learn. In looking at painting we discover not only what paintings are, we also discover ourselves, and the situation in which we live.

In Berger's intellectual universe, art and the world coexist onto-logically. Art goes to the very heart of our being, of our existence. Art is somehow central to our well-being, to our understanding of ourselves. Art is political and economic, too, needless to say, even if the development of art, its historical dynamics, can never be reduced simply to politics, nor to economics: art can never be beholden to either politics or economics. But the task of the seeing eye, especially the *critical* seeing eye, which Berger first enunciated in the 1950s in his brilliant, outspoken *New Statesman* columns (gaining him as many enemies as admirers), and in books like *Permanent Red*, *A Painter of Our Time* and *Ways of Seeing*, is both revolutionary and educational. It is 'to start a process of questioning', to loosen the bourgeois stranglehold on the history of art, on art as an exclusive domain of the rich. It is to let ordinary people enter into art history, to let them look and think critically and independently about painting and visual images.

Berger's great skill is to make art accessible without compromising intellectual rigour. Anybody can read his essays and books, take meaning from them. Anybody can use what they learn, use what they already know, even if they never quite knew it, in their own everyday lives. Berger manages to talk critically about art without ever spoiling the need to see great art, to see great pictures for oneself, in both galleries and books. His critical eye never vitiates the desire to appreciate art. Critically understanding art, he suggests, can only ever aid the pleasure of art. He has the distinct advantage here of never being a university prof, of never being crippled by wooden language, by 'academic' (in the worst sense of the term) point-scoring, by jargon and career pretensions. He has been refreshingly free of methodological straitjackets and of the need to defend such-and-such a school of thought.

But neither does Berger see himself as a *professional* art critic. This isn't so much self-deprecation as a paean to unaccommodated and un-co-opted amateurism, to his sense of free-floating outsiderness. Whatever circles he frequents, Berger always considers himself a rank amateur, an amateur as Edward Said construed an intellectual's true 'vocation'. (Said, remember, defined 'professionalism' as 'thinking of your work as something you do for a living, between the hours of nine and five with one eye on the clock, and another cocked at what is considered to be proper, professional behavior – not rocking the boat, making yourself marketable and above all presentable, hence uncontroversial and unpolitical.'[3]) For Berger, art criticism is not a real trade, is not a proper profession. It is not a real métier like, say, that of a literary critic, who uses words to represent other words, words to criticize the written word. With art the relationship is not commensurate: words can never adequately represent images, can never suitably portray on the page with any pen what has already been said on a canvas with a brush.

The eye moves faster and more probingly than the pen. But Berger, a trained painter, knows the painter's craft, knows the smell and disorderly feel of an artist's studio; he knows the complexity of the painter's mind, their grubby stained fingers, and this doubtless helps him find the occasional *mot juste* in his mind's eye. He has often said he has no verbal gifts, no musical ear, because what he sees before he writes are vivid images. His vocabulary is image-based, image-driven: he paints his words, layers them on, mixes colours on his writing tablet . . .

When, at the age of sixteen, Berger ran away from a sadistic boarding school in Oxford, from the 'monstrous' St Edward's, all he wanted to do in life was paint. His father, Stanley, a management admini-strator, director of the small and not very influential Institute of Costs and Works Accountants, was an upright, trustworthy man, a good administrator, who saw his eldest son, John (Berger has a brother, Michael, four years his junior), as civil servant material, or as dutifully engaged in a dependable profession like teaching school.[4] Stanley, after some initial conflict, later accepted his son's freelance desire to paint and write. He was irrevocably marked, father Stanley, by four years in the trenches as an infantry major; in civilian life he was a lost soul, never able to talk about his harrowing wartime experiences. Raised a non-observant Jew, prior to the First World War he had converted and entered a seminary to become a Catholic priest. But in 1914, says Berger, 'he left the seminary to volunteer. And after the war he decided he couldn't become a priest. He was so lost that he stayed in the Army for another four years organizing war graves'; until, that is, he met Berger's mother, a working-class woman from Lambeth, a suffragette and vegetarian, who saved Stanley. Since his birth, she wanted her son to be a writer.

After escaping from St Edward's Berger enrolled at London's Central School of Art and Design, interrupted by military service in the Ox and Bucks Light Infantry, where, as an ex-public school-boy, he refused an officer's commission. For his rebellion he was dispatched to Ballykelly, Northern Ireland, living among raw, working-class recruits. (His first brush with the lower classes, a brush that was to endure.) Afterwards, on a modest army scholarship, he returned to art school, this time to Chelsea College of Art, a formative experience spent 'painting, drawing, writing, and talking to Henry Moore', who taught Berger. 'Life was suddenly so full', said the young outsider.

At the time he was thin, almost slight. His shoulders and chest had not yet broadened. He read Brecht, Camus and Peter Kropotkin, rode motorbikes. He lived near Monmouth and shot rabbits. He visited the Soviet Union and East Germany. Everybody assumed he was a Communist Party member and he never denied it. (He was never a card-carrier.) He was mad about women but very shy. Few people would have recognized his shyness, for he had a passionately dogmatic way of talking, which concealed 'a multitude of hesitations'. The poet he most admired then – perhaps still most admires – was the Turkish Marxist Nâzim Hikmet, whose poems 'contained more space than any poetry I had until then read. They didn't describe space; they came through it, they crossed mountains. They were also about action. They related doubts, solitude, bereavement, sadness, but these feelings followed actions rather than being a substitute for action.'[5]

Berger continued to paint and draw (he would always draw), and taught art part-time. Yet to earn a living he began writing art criticism and doing journalism, scribbling precocious polemical pieces for the *New Statesman* (and later for *New Society*), dissent - ing pieces, and he met George Orwell along the way. He quickly adopted the Orwellian style: he asserted, sometimes at the gut or emotional level, and then proceeded to argue conceptually around that assertion, inside that assertion. 'Until 1954, I'd only ever thought of being a painter, but I earned my money when and where I could. You could say I drifted into writing.'

Soon Berger turned on his old teacher Henry Moore, denouncing the latter in print, creating a mini-drama in the British art world.

(*New Statesman* readers wrote in to complain; the British Council telephoned Moore personally to apologize for Berger's transgressions.) Moore's sculptures, wrote Berger in 1955 (5 November – his 29th birthday),

> reveal nothing about the way a body moves, grows or is controlled. They don't, in other words, take us *beyond* static appearances . . . Moore's distorted forms appear more immutable than any living appearances. They are dead? Not quite. More dead than alive? Yes, but what is more dead than alive? Inorganic matter . . . It is an art which has involuntarily put its back against the ultimate wall. Which is also why no one can follow Moore. One can't go further back than he has.[6]

Berger's real teachers, teachers that never physically taught him in any classroom, were middle-European Marxists, Marxist émigrés, political refugees from fascism, people like Austrian Ernst Fischer and Hungarian Frederick Antal, art critics whom he befriended in the 1950s – during the depths of the Cold War and nuclear threat. Each man showed how an open, Popular Front Marxism, a 'Prague Spring' Marxism, could enrich art criticism; neither brooked the traditional party line, especially the official Soviet Party line. Yet their rejections of Eastern Bloc dogmatism never equated to a rejection of socialism, nor of Marxism, because neither in the USSR bore any resemblance to the humanist Marxism they advocated.

Fischer's *The Necessity of Art* (1963), put into English by Anya Bostock, framed art much as Berger would frame art: around two different aspects of the self. One part is violent, hot, romantic, perhaps even extremist; the other sceptical, more distant, more cerebral, cooler. One is close up and angry, intoxicated and inspired, magical and Dionysian; the other steps back, gains distance, is an onlooker, an Apollonian analyst. The 'essential function of art for a class destined to change the world', Fischer wrote, 'is not that of *making magic* but of *enlightening* and *stimulating action*; it is equally true that a magical residue in art cannot be entirely eliminated, for without that minute residue of its original nature, art ceases to be art.'

The other aspect of art Fischer homed in on, and wrote brilliantly about, was the thorny relationship between 'form' and 'content'; on reading the bulky centrepiece chapter of *The Necessity of Art* you are struck by how much Berger's own form and content of art criticism has been influenced by Fischer's.

Any ruling class, Fischer says, profits from hiding the *content* of its class domination. The ruling classes rarely speak of the content of capitalist society: all they tend to do is extol the virtues of its democratic *form*. This, as Fischer points out, is *mystification*, blatant obfuscation, done to divert attention away from the real issue. In art something similar happens, and with the same debilitating political effects. Just as Marx in *Capital* famously spoke of how commodities become fetishized at the marketplace, becoming 'a definite social relation between men that assumes the fantastic form of a relation between things', there is a tendency in bourgeois circles to 'fetishize' form in art, to lay emphasis on its essential thing-like quality, on its 'pure' form, on its *eternal*, quintessential reality.

But the spirit of social criticism comes about precisely through prising open content, putting content in its necessary social and historical context, understanding how, for example, Brueghel painted scenes from a nascent bourgeois capitalism, how Millet depicted the misery and dreariness of the proletarian peasant, and how Van Gogh, Millet's unofficial pupil, took the peasant plight even further, painting their solitude, their wretched and twisted bodies, their exhaustion; and how Diego Rivera did likewise with degraded Mexican workers, while also pillorying their antagonists, the Spanish oppressors, the comprador ruling class.

It almost goes without saying that emphasis on content complicates art, makes it contested terrain, subjective. It means that art is determined not so much by what a painting depicts as 'by how it does so: how the artist, consciously or unconsciously, expresses the social tendencies of his time.' To interpret the content of a painting, Fischer says, 'is sometimes a difficult undertaking, and contradictory conclusions can be drawn.' What external forces, what influences peculiar to his or her time is any artist obeying? Are they overpowered by their own unconscious? Does the meaning they want to put into the work conceal a deeper one, a meaning that is, in the final analysis, social?

Berger's other early *maître*, Frederick Antal, seems to have been something of a political role model for Janos Lavin, the fictional lead of *A Painter of Our Time*, Berger's debut novel, published in 1958 – a book, incidentally, that marked Berger's adieu to art, to his youthful ambitions of being a painter. (Even though Berger was an image man, he realized that words were greater weapons in political struggle.) Like Lavin, Antal was from Budapest, a contemporary of Georg Lukács and a humanist-communist.[7] Lavin and Antal both studied law and intended to be lawyers; both left Hungary in 1919 after the overthrow by the Soviet revolutionary government; both men hated two things with almost equal passion: the class system and the official Communist line on art.

Antal was an art historian rather than a practising artist. He studied in Vienna, Berlin and Paris, spent several years in Florence studying fourteenth-century Italian painting (later penning *Florentine Painting and its Social Background*), and eventually, upon fleeing the Nazis, again like Lavin, settled in London in the 1930s. Antal befriended Anthony Blunt, the director of the Courtauld Institute of Art, and lectured at the same institution until his death in 1954. Of Antal, Berger himself says:

He set out to show in detail how sensitive painting was to economic and ideological developments. Single-handed he disclosed, with all the rigour of a European scholar, a new seam of content in pictures, and through this seam ran the class struggle. But I do not think that he believed that this explained the phenomenon of art. His respect for art was such that he could not forgive, as Marx could not forgive, the history he studied.

Doubtless Antal's Marxism suffered the same mix of bourgeois heckles and vehement vilification that Berger's *A Painter of Our Time* received shortly after its public airing. Each man was a communist spy, a Soviet sympathizer, a threat to the 'free' world, right? Stephen Spender, writing in *The Observer*, said Berger's book 'stank of the concentration camps' and could only have been written by one other man: Josef Goebbels![8] (This wasn't necessarily *The Observer*'s own view: in the same broadsheet, Ken Tynan thought *A Painter of Our Time* a book of the year.) The irony with Spender's claim was that Berger's book emerged out of the very *experience* of living with European political refugees, invariably Jewish refugees, those escaping fascism. Berger was even in Prague in the summer of 1968 when the Soviet tanks rolled in; he was there to give messages of support from the West for supporters of Dubček!

Berger's empathy for the 'European' intellectual was paramount in his desire to quit Britain. Perhaps there was an atavism? His father's father, after all, was from Trieste, one of James Joyce's staging posts. Or maybe there was a push factor, such as English cynicism, legendary in its own right; or terrible weather, always a spur to flee Blighty for warmer climes. Perhaps, above all else, it was English *philistinism*? Pain, thinks Berger, is the starting point of all English philistinism; for the English, pain is somehow 'undignified': the stiff upper lip, the refusal of pain, the denial of pain, the English emotional cripple, unable to talk seriously about feelings without embarrassment, without belittling, cynical jokes . . .

Berger's complicity with the European intellectual, with the Continental European temperament, 'grew from the assumption that pain is at the source of human imagination. This didn't make us solemn – but it did make us embrace, make us put our arms around one another – to the embarrassment of any watching Englishman.'[9] The complicity also grew because of a will to be unashamedly intellectual, to be unashamedly *intense*. 'Why did you want to leave England?' somebody once asked Berger. 'I'd wanted to leave England since I was about 18', he answered. 'I didn't really feel at home there. So often I had the feeling when I was with people, when I spoke, that I embarrassed them. I think because they considered me *indecently intense*.'[10]

When 'Ways of Seeing' was first broadcast in January 1972, Berger's relationship with the *institution* of art, while well established (he had been a frequent presenter on Huw Wheldon's BBC *Monitor* art series, 1958–65), was nonetheless a bit like another European's – Caravaggio, his favourite artist – which is to say, tense and difficult, full of a certain cocky disdain. Caravaggio was equally indecently intense. 'There are nobler painters', Berger admits in his essay 'Caravaggio' (*Studio International*, 1983), 'and painters of greater breadth of vision. There are painters I admire more and who are more admirable. But there is none . . . to whom I feel closer.'[11]

Like Caravaggio Berger treated – still treats – the rarefied world of dealers and experts, of curators and tweedy connoisseurs, with a good deal of contempt. 'The complicity I feel with Caravaggio', he says, 'began in Livorno during the late 1940s', a city then war-scarred and dirt poor. 'Caravaggio was the first painter of life as experienced by the *popolaccio*, the people of the back streets, *les sans-culottes*, the lumpenproletariat, the lower orders, those of the lower depths, the underworld.' In discovering Caravaggio, finding him in Livorno, 'I first began to learn something about the ingenuity of the dispossessed. It was there too that I discovered

Looking intense.

that I wanted as little as possible to do in this world with those who wield power. This has turned out to be a life-long aversion.'

In a strange sense, the relationship of Caravaggio – and his affinity with outcasts, with rough-handed labourers, with peasants with dirty feet, with a soiled and sordid life – to Nicolas Poussin, who rested his case on ideal beauty, perfect form and classical decorum, bore a stark likeness to Berger's relationship to one Kenneth Clark. His bushy hairdo in 'Ways of Seeing', his open-necked chainmail shirt, his eyeballing of the audience, his beguiling pale blue eyes – seducer's eyes – his pointing fingers, questioning stance, driven and feisty style, said it all, set the programme's radical tonality; it shared a certain complicity with Caravaggio's own vernacular, to his rougher and 'dirtier' style.

For 'Civilization' Clark had visited eleven countries, 117 locations and 118 museums, roaming the world in search of the 'original' when all he could let everybody see, on their TV screens, was its reproduction. In 'Ways of Seeing' Berger visited only two museums: London's National Gallery and another, a fake museum, a makeshift studio in Ealing, where he took out a knife and proceeded to cut out Venus's head from Botticelli's *Venus and Mars*. So began the dramatic, combative introduction of one of the most influential art series ever to hit the small screen. (There were tenderer moments, to be sure, when Berger visited a primary school in south London, patiently asking kids to comment on *Supper at Emmaus*, Caravaggio's sexually ambivalent vision of Jesus.)

On television, in front of the camera, Berger's spiel seemed entirely spontaneous. Yet it had been meticulously scripted behind the scenes, edited and reedited, shaped and reshaped through trial and error, through dialogue and collaborative critique, especially with director Mike Dibb. Berger, Dibb says, is not naturally gifted at ad-libbing on screen. So he read from an autocue, which, at Dibb's insistence, was speeded up to give Berger's slow, pensive diction more pace, more of a punchier feel, more Caravaggio red.

Such rawness, such savvy professionalism, begot a sort of unselfconscious amateurism, all of which was part of the infectious charm of 'Ways of Seeing', part of its compelling success. Jean-Luc Godard was an obvious inspiration – particularly for Mike Dibb; Helmut Herzfelde, aka John Heartfield, an early pioneer of photomontage and friend of Brecht, was another. Both Godard and Heartfield had shown how you can be *formally* bold with ideas, that ideas can be filmic as well as dramatic, animated as well as inspirational; dare to try! Each of the four programmes gives the impression of being made up, of being scripted and filmed on the hoof, winged spontaneously as you go along: the programmes really were journeys of discovery, for the production team as well as the audience. That's presumably what gives 'Ways of Seeing' its *zap*, its high-octane feel: Berger's super-brainy charisma juxtaposed to a dancing Pan's People, to Biba babes posing for *Vogue*. Who could have conceived such a magic potion in advance?

Mike Dibb, who would collaborate with Berger on other television documentaries in the 1980s and '90s, admits as much: 'although "Ways of Seeing" may appear to be a succession of statements, these statements are really questions. When John speaks in conversation his sentences often end with an interrogative. "No?" he says, inviting a response, not automatic assent.' This is also true of his letters:

> Dear Mike, Here's script no. 2. Please remember all I said about it on the phone. Criticize, improvise, change, improve, cancel out, as much as you want or see how to. Or even we can begin again. All I would stand by is the essential idea about ownership and its reversed function with the advent of the consumer society.

As a postscript, Berger adds, scribbling in Geneva late Friday night, winter 1971: 'I think the commentary in the script should be far more

Friday night

Genève
—.

Dear Mike,

Here's the script no. 2.

Please remember all I said about it on the phone. Criticize, improvise, change, improve, cancel out, as much as you wish or see how to. Or even we can begin again. All I would stand by is the essential idea about ownership and its reversed function with the advent of the consumer society. Can't write tonight. Every word disobeys.

my very best wishes —
as now

John.

—.

I think the commentary in the script should be far more questioning, suggestive: less didactic / dogmatic. But I have made it like this to make it clear in my mind.

Berger letter to Mike Dibb, winter 1971.

questioning, suggestive: less didactic/dogmatic. But I have made it like this to make it clear in my mind.'

Such is exemplary of Berger's approach to collaboration, of how he thrived off it, still thrives off it: collaborations with photographers (Jean Mohr), with filmmakers (Robert Vas, Mike Dibb, Alain Tanner, Timothy Neat), with writers and translators (Nella

Bielski, Anne Michaels, daughter Katya, Rema Hammami, Anya Bostock), with artists (son Yves, John Christie, Marisa Camino) and with theatre directors (Simon McBurney). 'The important thing about collaboration', he says,

> is not to make compromises. All differences of opinion have to be faced, reflected on. It's like the opposite of committees, where people are swamped by compromises. Mike Dibb remains a close friend. We had this idea of making a four-programme series about the relationship between art and image. It was very low budget, not important to anyone, so no one was on our backs. We spent six or eight months working on it. The BBC didn't believe in it and showed it very late at night. The book came as a hurried add-on.[12]

The point of departure of 'Ways of Seeing', the 'essential idea' for its form, is Walter Benjamin's essay 'The Work of Art in the Age of Mechanical Reproduction'. Written in 1938, this brilliant and very dense essay appeared in the US in 1968 under Hannah Arendt's caring tutelage. It had seeped across the Atlantic a couple of years later and Berger had read it, been stimulated by it and responded to its challenge: how to translate it into accessible TV, into a popular arts series, particularly for the concluding programme? Apparently Berger and Dibb were not too sure about the content of their fourth and final show. Then, so it goes, early one evening, on his way to dine with Huw Wheldon, Berger had a brainwave on the London Underground.

He had seen ads on the escalators and walls. He had noticed how many advertisers were making direct references in their publicity to works of art from the past. The poses of fashion models somehow reflected the poses of models in Classical art; colour photography bore an uncanny resemblance to the glossy texturing of oil painting. Where was the tradition of oil painting reconstituting itself? In advertising: in the desire and seduction and status of elite culture made 'popular'. The ad men were using artistic images to help sell their products. As the assembled images in 'Ways of Seeing' tried to show (images assembled by Mike Dibb from hordes of fashion magazines), very often ads were flagrant pastiches of well-known paintings whose iconography was being co-opted and redeployed as marketing tropes, with vivid colour photography assuming the function that oil paint once had. One conclusion could be drawn: art of the past no longer exists as it once did. Its authority is lost.

The mechanical reproduction of a work of art, Benjamin says, represents something new. The advent of photography and film has transformed cultural life and artistic production, transformed the very act of looking itself, the seeing eye, which now sees more things than it once did, sees them quicker than before, more precisely than ever. Yet it sees them refracted through the lens of a camera, on pages of a magazine, on giant billboards, in ever-shifting scenes. And this has new powers of deceit, new powers of persuasion. The possibility to infinitely reproduce a work of art means that art lacks uniqueness. The original hangs somewhere, still lives on, and continues to merit viewing; but 'technical repro-duction', Benjamin says, 'can put the copy of the original into situations which would be out of the reach for the original itself.'

The concept of authenticity has lost its authentic meaning. The 'aura' of a work of art has withered in the age of mechanical repro-duction. The technique of reproduction 'detaches the reproduced object from the domain of tradition'. All of this, for Benjamin as well as for Berger, is epochal in its historical reach, epochal in its progressive possibilities. But it is equally epochal in its new threats, in its new ambushes, in new forms of commodification and market penetration. With the aura gone, the work of art has lost its God-given property, its pure 'naturalness'. Art is no longer an 'ominous idol', Benjamin says, no longer an object of veneration, an expression of cult. Art's holiness has now been rendered profane, its halo stripped away. 'For the first time in world history', Benjamin writes, 'mechanical reproduction emancipates the work of art from its parasitical dependence on ritual.'

This is the good news; and here Berger and Benjamin agree on the progressive implications. Instead of being based on ritual, art begins on another practice: *politics*. The loss of aura, the loss of art's halo, means that art can now be embedded in its rightful context: the messy reality of everyday social relations. Berger knew how the bourgeois art establishment struggled to keep intact art's aura, struggled to defend it in its own class interests. He still knows it. Some of the most powerful moments of 'Ways of Seeing' occur when Berger tries to expose this sort of mystification. Take Frans Hals's two great paintings, *Regents of the Old Men's Alms House* and *Regentesses of the Old Men's Alms House*: two officially commissioned portraits done in the winter of 1664, when the Dutch artist, then over 80, was destitute. If not for public charity letting Hals obtain three loads of peat, says a deadpan Berger, he would have frozen to death.

In front of Hals are the earnest and rather smug-looking men and women administrators of public charity, dressed in formal period garb. Are they painted in a spirit of bitterness? Berger wonders. In an authoritative study of Hals, Seymour Slive waxes lyrical about the *form* of the Regentesses:

> Each woman stands out with equal clarity against the enormous dark surface . . . Subtle modulations of the deep, glowing blacks contribute to the harmonious fusion of the whole and form an unforgettable contrast with powerful whites and vivid flesh tones where the detached strokes reach a peak of breadth and strength.

Compare Berger, confronting the above passage, using his own italics in the printed book, *Ways of Seeing*:

Here the composition is written about as though it were in itself the emotional charge of the painting. Terms like *harmonious fusion*, *unforgettable contrast*, reaching *a peak of breadth and strength* transfer the emotion provoked by the image from the plane of lived experience, to that of disinterested 'art appreciation'. All conflict disappears. One is left with the unchanging 'human condition', and the painting considered as a marvelously made object.

With the subsequent loss of aura, Berger believes art can now enter the mainstream, can now be consumed en masse, can now circulate more freely. Less specialized publics can see art, can question art, art in relation to their own lived experience, art in relation to the historical experience of their class or gender. Erstwhile narrow definitions of art are blasted open; art is wrestled out of the hands of a few select experts who, in Berger eyes, 'are the clerks of the nostalgia of a ruling class in decline'.

On the other hand, the mechanical reproduction of art also leads to an ever-greater fetishization of the original. Elite people now pay obscene amounts of money to possess an 'authentic' Van Gogh or Picasso. Elite people are able to profit more than ever on art as a scarce and monopolizable product, speculating on the art market much as they speculate on stocks and shares, possessing art merely to accumulate capital. Meanwhile art reproductions become mass-produced commodities sold at every museum book - store, hung on every bedroom and living room wall, produced on postcards and key-rings, on T-shirts and in sales promotions.

Though with this popularization come new opportunities, for art to be politicized rather than purely aestheticized. In this sense, *Ways of Seeing* identifies the same capitalist dialectic in art that Marx's *Communist Manifesto* identifies in bourgeois society, leaving us all in a strange and paradoxical position. 'All fixed, fast-frozen relationships', Marx says, 'with their train of venerable ideas and opinions, are swept away. All that is solid melts into air, all that is holy is profaned, and men at last are forced to face with sober senses the real conditions of their lives and their relations with their fellow men.' Capitalism has *de-sanctified* social life, art included: through its product innovation, through its insatiable development dynamic, capitalism has perversely democratized art by commodifying art. We can now all pretty much appreciate art, with sober senses, as only a cultured minority once did. What we do in the future with that appreciation, with the knowledge of ourselves that we can glean from great art, remains, Berger says at the end of *Ways of Seeing*, to be seen. It is another question that's 'to be continued . . .'

Ways of Seeing encountered plenty of nay-sayers, needless to say, plenty of thumbs down from the art establishment, from the old-guard, from vested art interests; Berger's take is too simplistic, some said, too moralistic; *Ways of Seeing* can't say anything meaningful about today's 'modern' art; his performance is too theatrical, too confrontational for soberer tastes, is marred by a residue of 1960s radicalism, of dogmatism, etc., etc.; the text is too hastily written, too slapdash . . .

Within the critical fold there were also detractors. The late Peter Fuller, for instance, argued that his former mentor had given us a sort of 'left idealist' interpretation of art. Fuller's pamphlet *Seeing Berger: A Revaluation of Ways of Seeing* (1980), was an aggressive, Oedipal attack, an attempt to kill the father. Berger's *Ways of Seeing*, Fuller maintained, lacked a sufficiently 'materialist theory of expression', and so cannot adequately distinguish between original paintings and works of reproduction – tellingly confirmed by the poor quality of the (reproduced) photos in the book. Fuller said that in Berger one could spot the same split that tore apart Walter Benjamin: on the one side a historical materialist, progressive, 'technist' position which praises new media, and on the other a spiritual, aesthetic stance, the latter largely operating in a sealed-off enclave. Hence the two perspectives are never reconciled.

In a personal letter to Fuller dated 11 June 1980, Berger was surprisingly gracious:

> I have read your essay and I think it is *very good*. Its arguments are just and clear, and they correct what is false in *Ways of Seeing*, as well as going beyond it . . . I never considered *Ways of Seeing* an important work: it was a *partial*, polemical reply – as you say. But it became 'important' because it has been read and used . . . The reproductions are bad in *Ways of Seeing*, *not* as a matter of principle, but because we insisted in our publishing contract that the book must sell (at that time) for less than £1. It was cheaper, thanks to our insistence, than any comparable popular art book. Of course this *cheapness* was part of its theoretical thrust (and of its theoretical over-simplifications). [Berger's emphases.]

The cheapness also gave it its relative freedom, the freedom that art has gained in the age of mechanical reproduction, a freedom that enabled a programme like 'Ways of Seeing' to become a low-budget hit in the first place, travelling nowhere yet saying bundles everywhere. But just as it opened up a niche, just as 'Ways of Seeing' pioneered one future direction of television arts programming, a radical direction, the doors began to close; the parameters of a specifically market freedom narrowed, just as Marx's *Manifesto* prophesied. 'You couldn't make programmes like "Ways of Seeing" today', Berger commented in 1994. 'You wouldn't be given that sort of freedom.'[13]

And it is true, perhaps even truer now, circa 2012: the success of 'Ways of Seeing' belonged to a special moment of making television arts programmes, and that moment, that era, no longer exists. The current BBC has enough archive material from their old hit show to mean that it is cheaper and more convenient to mechanically reproduce 'Ways of Seeing', to occasionally repeat it and rerun it, than to risk something completely new, risk upsetting middle management, those who were not even born when chainmail shirts were all the rage . . .

One of the most innovative art essays Berger ever wrote would cue, in the early 1970s, his most ambitious novelistic undertaking. That essay, 'The Moment of Cubism' (1969), revisited a theme he had first broached in book form in 1965, through the lens of the movement's great innovator, Picasso (cf. *The Success and Failure of Picasso*). In 'The Moment of Cubism' Berger emphasizes the historical conjuncture of Cubist art, its historical 'moment'. Cubism, he thinks, was responsive to, as well as responsible for, dramatic changes in the culture of time and space, beginning roughly in 1880 and flourishing until the outbreak of the Great War.

Sweeping inventions and innovations in technology (electricity, wireless telegraph, telephones, cinema, Ford Model T mass-produced cars, and ships, for example the *Titanic*), in science (Einstein's relativity theory, quantum physics, Freud's psychoanalysis) and in culture (atonal music, jazz, Joyce and Proust in literature) ushered in a 'new way of seeing' that Cubism helped both glimpse and create. Thus Cubism, says Berger, 'shared the same determinants' as these other movements, dialectically positioned itself within them, within a specific historical conjuncture it was in part making. 'I hear the ruin of all space', Joyce wrote in *Ulysses*, 'shattered glass and toppling masonry', and Picasso, that arch-creator and destroyer, concurred.

Picasso was a genius, Berger says, but like all geniuses he was a product as well as a pioneer of his time. His prodigious gifts, his 'natural' gifts, were also Spanish gifts, specifically southern Spanish gifts, fused by libertarian anarchism and ignited by *duende*, the undiabolic demon Picasso's poet countryman, Frederico García

Lorca, consecrated. *Duende*, said Lorca, burns in the blood like a poultice of broken glass. It leans on pain and smashes styles. All great artists of southern Spain, whether they sing or dance, bullfight or paint, know, if they know anything at all, that nothing comes unless the *duende* comes. 'The duende is the inspired cry of defiance', Berger says in *The Success and Failure of Picasso* (1965), 'of those on the rack. It is the impatience to have done, to break free from all material beginnings which appear never to develop: it is the attempt to transcend those beginnings by abandoning everything to the moment.'

Hence the moment of Cubism burned with all the ecstatic passion of the *duende*. To the Cubists, to Picasso and Braque, to Juan Gris and Léger, Cubism was utterly spontaneous; to Berger it was part of history, a changing history, an unfinished history. It was a dialectical moment rather than a stylistic category, dialectical materialism brought to canvas, framed geometrically. The Cubists groped their way along, picture by picture, towards a new synthesis. This new synthesis in painting was really the pictorial equivalent of a concurrent revolution in scientific thinking, in theoretical physics. If the human eye could perceive quantum theory, it would somehow resemble *Woman with a Mandolin*, or *Man with a Pipe*. To understand its antecedent, relativity theory, perhaps we should look no further than *Les Demoiselles d'Avignon*.

What the eye sees is a shifting state of nature, when all is process and flux, when all matter is both a particle and a wave. The moment of Cubism is when we, as passive observers, actively participate in the five-dimensional reality unfolding before us. Like a scene from *The Exorcist*, we see heads turning 360 degrees, view somebody's back from the front. Static entities suddenly move through time before our very eyes, and we move with them. Like the objects being portrayed, we, too, are in several places at once; we are unnerved, dislocated. We are forced to look anew at what a painting is, at who we are, at where we were and where we're headed. 'Cubism is an art', Berger explains in 'The Moment of Cubism',

> entirely concerned with interaction: the interaction between different aspects: the interaction between structure and movement: the interaction between solids and the space around them: the interaction between the unambiguous signs made on the surface of a picture and the changing reality which they stand in for.

The definition Berger coined, a surprisingly clunky one, was *interjacent*: a dynamic sort of interaction, the idea that the space between objects becomes part of the objects' own identity, that sheer relationships themselves become visible to the senses; the staging of any drama henceforth becomes part of the script, part of the action. Cubes float before our eyes, shimmer in a dynamic process of stream-of-consciousness montage; realism now somehow becomes surreal; naturalism is denatured, no longer mirroring our world but instead transformed into a series of *diagrammatic* representations of our world. Discontinuity on canvas signals discontinuity of the self; Freud knew as much; and in 1972 an 'interjacency' in art would soon make it to the page, would find its creative form in another way of seeing Berger, a more experimental modernist John Berger: the moment of *G*.

2

G. and Un-*G.*

'The power of colour is nothing compared to the power of the line.'
Janos Lavin in *A Painter of Our Time*

'I write in the spirit of a geometrician.'
John Berger, *G.*

What a strange novel *G.* is, what a strange tapestry Berger penned
there. Penned, yes, not painted, because this 'deliberate collage' –
as George Steiner once called it – is not done in paint and with
colours but with lines and full stops, with all the precision of a
geometrician. Has anyone noticed how few commas there are in
G.? Commas, after all, introduce ambiguity, make sentences curve,
bend off from the straight and narrow, create vagueness, make
meaning pliable; commas add clauses and only make compromises
and *G.*, if nothing else, is an *un*compromising book, a book of
pure narration, a book that would dramatically make amends for
Berger's two prior novelistic flops, *The Foot of Clive* (1962) and
Corker's Freedom (1964).[1]
　　The central character in *G.* is himself uncompromising, likewise
defined by a full stop, by a .; and that dot somehow protects his
identity, ensures that Berger's hero can only ever be an anti-hero,
a protagonist who rarely speaks, who is hardly any protagonist at
all. It is not until well over a hundred pages in that we first learn
his name, that the name G. is spoken aloud by its creator. We

almost never hear G. think, nor do we listen to his emotional life; and it is hard for anybody, any reader, to like this testosterone-charged, leering, gap-toothed lad who can't control his own modern sexuality, fucking his way across Europe. (A childhood riding accident knocked out his two front teeth and created that leer.) His dick would be his eventual undoing, and somehow we guess this in advance, as he chases just one too many women at the onset of the Great War.

G. may be a Cubist novel but the central subject is made up of only two dimensions. G. has no depth, no anchorage anywhere, no roots, no fixed identity, nothing to pivot on, nothing that interacts with any context. He is utterly free-floating. He is not obstinate, we hear, because obstinacy is defensive: it is always deployed around a fixed citadel. Neither is he a dreamer. He isn't anything, really, other than rather ugly, a man without evident qualities; and yet he is the biggest gigolo anybody has known since Casanova, since Don Juan, since Giovanni, his namesake. He is totally devastating with women, and seems totally devastating *for* women, their liberator. Unlike other men, one female admirer says, he has convinced me that his desire for me – for me alone – is absolute, that it is *her existence* that has created his desire. He gives the impression that he is there only to satisfy women, that he is selfless in his sexuality, that the organism is hers, just hers.

What's his secret? Nobody quite knows. It lurks incognito behind the dot; Berger is coy. He makes G. Teflon: the truth slips off him, nothing sticks. Who is he, what are his interests? 'I travel', G. says, with typical irony. He's like Gilles, the thinly disguised Guy Debord character from Michèle Bernstein's novel *Tous les chevaux du roi*. 'What do you work as? How do you occupy your time?' 'I wander', retorts Gilles, 'mainly, I wander . . .'. Like Gilles, the other G. is the arch-nemesis of reification: he strips it away, gets right to the core of things, without mediation, without preservatives. He's not into stockings: he cuts right to the flesh, to bare legs. His penis is his trusty weapon of demystification: it hits the spot, the bull's-eye, each time. It's a rod from which his legs dangle down either side; he rides his great wand: it has wings.

Signed off – in a *clin d'œil privé* to James Joyce's *Ulysses* – 'Geneva–Paris–Bonnieux, 1965–1971', a 40-something Berger was then as seemingly peripatetic as his rootless half-Italian, half-English seducer. Formally the book is genius, brilliantly conceived, imaginative and sexy and intriguing, a work of great modernism, executed by a master modernist craftsman, meriting every accolade, every prize. The language is razor-sharp; sentences are clean, chiselled. Poetic fragments hinting of Mallarmé, Ovid and Hölderlin are juxtaposed with historical documentation; the author himself qualifies his philosophical digressions, his metaphysical ruminations, frequently intervening in the narrative flow, offering detailed explication and moral justification.

Berger's creation is full of the same intelligence, full of the same high-minded modernist mannerism of, say, Milan Kundera's *The Unbearable Lightness of Being*, with its G.-like counterpart, the philandering doctor Tomas; Laclos's devilish womanizer Vicomte de Valmont in *Dangerous Liaisons* equally comes to mind. And so, too, does Ulrich, the eponymous anti-hero of Robert Musil's *The Man Without Qualities*, the Austrian Musil who passed his last years in Geneva admiring, as Berger admired penning many lines of *G.*, the massive limestone monolith Mont Salève, which shadows Rousseau's fair city. Ulrich and G. each follow Musil's pet metaphor of 'flypaper': humans are like flies, irresistibly attracted by sweet-smelling flypaper. We can't help ourselves, we love its sweet-stickiness, the lure of its sensual odour; yet just as the fly is doomed upon contact, we too are doomed: no matter how much we wriggle, no matter how much we try to break free, here's no escape.

George Steiner was the first critic to stress the lineage between Musil's Ulrich and G. The two novels, he wrote in *The New Yorker* (see 'Gamesmen', 27 January 1973), justifying his decision to award Berger the 1972 Booker Prize, share something important in common: they both invent essentially passive heroes at the intersection of real historical crises, of economic, political and psychological crises, at turning points in European history. Steiner said Berger had given us a very *un*English novel, which is doubtless why it has so many English detractors, so many antagonists. (Auberon Waugh in *The Spectator* called it an 'imbecilic book'; meanwhile *The Sunday Express* thought *G.* a 'trendy mockery of a novel'.)

Steiner liked *G.* because it spoke to his own high-modernist sensibilities, to his own cerebral peregrinations: Steiner is a deracinated, Jewish middle-European polyglot, an intellectual émigré whose family made it to Paris (and later to New York) before the Nazis stomped into town. (He once said, thank God he didn't have roots. Trees have roots, Steiner thought, not people, who have legs. He owed his life to his legs. Steiner calls himself a 'grateful wanderer'. If he'd not been able to move, to run, he'd be dead today.) Legend has it that Steiner had a clear run among the Booker judges. His other colleagues, Cyril Connolly and Elizabeth Bowen, offered little input: the former was usually inebriated for the judging meetings, while the latter absented herself because of illness. Thus Steiner could opt for whomever he wished, choosing Berger for his artistry, for his dialectical experimentation, for his originality and inventiveness; *G.*, Steiner concluded, defied Kierke-gaard's insistence that music, not words, is only ever capable of capturing the true spirit of Eros.

G. was conceived through an unlikely encounter between a rich, overweight fruit merchant called Umberto, from Livorno, Caravaggio's home town, and a 26-year-old American woman called Laura, a podgy divorcée attracted for God knows what reason to the married Italian. They have nothing in common, yet Laura becomes Umberto's steady mistress on his travels; somehow the two liberate one another. Umberto has a kind heart but he is a conservative with reactionary tendencies. He hates crowds: the crowd is at best remote and abstract, Umberto says, and at worst insane and rabid. A sane man should always see himself apart from the masses, apart from the crowd; he should always see himself as an exemption from the rest of the world.

Laura, on the other hand, believes that the individual should never kowtow to the demands of any conventional morality. So when she's pregnant with G., knowing Umberto is too cowardly to admit the awful truth to his wife, she tries to raise the kid herself. But wet nurses and governesses intervene between her and her illegitimate child; the latter is soon whisked off to the countryside, to a farm in the south of England run by Laura's English cousins, brother and sister pairing Jocelyn and Beatrice. Meanwhile, in London, mother Laura is converted to the Fabian socialist cause. She exits the stage, abandoning her child, suggesting the secret of life is now no longer hidden in her body but in the evolutionary political process; we hear nothing more of Laura's exploits. And for the large chunk of the book, 'the boy', as he is known, embarks upon a solitary rural existence, having the hots for his governess Miss Helen. He discovers the pleasures of adolescent sexual arousal, isolating the precise point of this mysteriously joyful stimulation: 'The mystery which inflames him and at night in bed stiffens his penis leads the boy to ask a number of questions.'

The boy learns to hunt, to ride a horse, to be a budding country gent, to amuse himself, alone. Jocelyn and Beatrice become surro-gate parents, until Beatrice marries an army officer; she goes off to South Africa where her masochistic husband is killed in the Boer War. Jocelyn broods his sister's absence, and the incestuous relationship is revealed. Then Beatrice returns to the farm, and seduces the boy. Berger gives us a rough sketch of his already impressive penis and her vagina. Aunt Beatrice is no longer contained within any contour: she's a continuous surface, she's something out of Dante, or maybe out of Mallarmé, his Beatrice, G.'s destruction, her destruction. Her skin is softer than the boy had previously imagined. He kisses her breast, takes her nipple in his mouth. She can't remember the lilac in her bedroom ever having a scent like that before . . .

Fast forward to G. the man, all grown up, fatter, more evidently his father's son, messing about in planes, messing about with young chambermaids in Swiss hotels. 'She fills my life', G. says of the young chambermaid. 'But we've only been here for a day', his friend Weymann quizzes. G. is now a rich dandy. He's aged, he's inherited his father's fortune, owning three factories, two cargo vessels and fifteen houses near the centre of Livorno. But he has no business sense and little inclination to work. Then the action switches to Domodossola, Italy, September 1910, where the Peruvian-Italian aviator Geo Chávez has just made history in a solo crossing of the Alps; the first man to fly what was previously thought impossible. But in a freak last-minute lapse, Chávez's plane suddenly dips upon landing and inexplicably crashes, breaking his legs. He may never walk again – though his life isn't in danger. Yet Chávez is haunted by the historic event, which is painstakingly and accurately documented by author B. The former's condition deteriorates; all Italy holds its breath, prays for a recovery. But Chávez slips away, just as G. is getting his leg over Camille, the exotic wife of Peugeot businessman Maurice Hennequin.

For Camille, G. spoke French terribly and didn't read a word of poetry; yet he could explain Mallarmé, her dear Mallarmé, whose poetry is inexplicable. G. is imprudent and impudent: 'I love you. How I love you', he tells Camille at a first meeting, a posh soirée in which one is meant to hold one's tongue, disguise one's feelings. 'You are beautiful. You have eyes which say everything. And you have a voice of a corn-crake.' Is that last remark a compliment? she wonders. Irrepressibly, he insists, 'I must see you tomorrow.'

So in a forest, alone with one another, Camille strips before him and 'sees herself as a dryad, alert in a way that is more animal than human, quick, sensitive, fleet-footed, soft-tongued, shameless'. She tastes herself in the flesh made of another. This can never stop, she slowly and calmly whispers. 'My love, my love . . .'. Still, Monsieur H., the cuckolded husband, is outraged when he discovers his wife's infidelities, especially with such a cad; everyone is outraged at G.'s fornications as Italy mourns their aviator's sad demise. If G. meddles again with his wife, Monsieur H. will shoot him. G., heedless and careless, continues to meddle, and receives a shoulder wound in a *crime passionnel*.

The denouement of *G.* has our man entangled in the liberation of Italy from Habsburg domination. Now in Trieste, G. gets mixed up with a group of Young Bosnians responsible for the assassination in Sarajevo of Archduke Franz Ferdinand, heir to the Habsburg throne, shot dead by Gavrilo Princip, the nineteen-year-old co-conspirator of a certain Bojan. Bojan is a young idealist Slav, a fearless activist with poetic pretensions. His sister is Nusa, a plump Slovene peasant girl, whom Bojan finds one day seated in a cemetery beside G., the object of the latter's curiosity. G. speaks Italian like an Italian, but the Young Bosnian suspects something untoward; he thinks G. might be a spy, an enemy infiltrator, and to some extent he's right. Now, at the behest of the British Foreign Office, G. strangely accepted a proposition to keep a close eye on Irredentist squabbles for Her Majesty's Government. He's in Trieste on a fake Italian passport – a passport Nusa dearly covets for her brother's underground activities. In the meantime G. is promised a night's mad passion with Marika, a Hungarian goddess, wife of the rich Austrian banker Wolfgang von Hartmann, promised by her banker husband himself after a charity ball.

The plot now thickens: characters and scenes start to inter-weave; things happen fast; there's dramatic tension because G. agrees to give Nusa his passport, to condemn himself, if she'll condemn herself and accompany him to the ball. All the while, Berger can't help wondering if G. is aware of the epic historical changes unfolding around him. Has he had a premonition of the changes, the author asks, changes that'll transform forever social life and death in Europe? 'I do not know', says 'B.', the narrator Berger in *G.* (let's call him B.). In any event, G. has no interest in either history or politics; his future seems only short-term, his pleasures only ever immediate and concrete.

His destiny is *now* and it's eternal, involving two women: the tall, stag-like Marika, and the simple, poor Nusa, the Slovene lass who moves like a carthorse. Imagine the scandal when G. arrives, arm in arm with the 'plate-licking' peasant, dressed in pearls and muslin and Indian silk. Guests gasp in horror. When they dance together, G. and Nusa, nobody will join them. Onlookers guffaw incredulously. Unable to control her consternation, Marika sets about Nusa with a horsewhip. The latter runs for her life. Several men advance upon G. The duo flees, is pursued through the streets. The police intervene and call the unlikely couple in for questioning and cross-questioning. Both are released.

G. has 36 hours to leave the country. He goes to see Nusa, for old times' sake, at her attic apartment. He hands over his passport. Street noises disturb them. Crowds gather outside. Italians declared war today, and we're at war with them, Nusa says. They exit and begin to walk with the crowd, in their direction. The crowd is erratic and haphazard. It attracts him like flypaper, as it had as a small boy in 1898 when, clutching the hand of a poor Roman girl, he'd been swept along in a mass demonstration of workers in Milan. In his white shirt, with his foreign mannerisms, his alien movements, the adult G. stands out amongst the crowd: he isn't one of them or one with it. He hasn't really given himself over to the crowd. He is singled out. They take him, march him away, whack him on the head. He faints. The taste of milk is the cloud of unknowing. He is lowered into the wavy salt water, dropped feet first into the canal . . .

Throughout Berger's *G.* years, one of his staple bedside reads was Georg Lukács' *The Theory of the Novel*.[2] The Hungarian Hegelian-Marxist wrote his famed study around the same time as the action of *G.* occurred, on the cusp of the Great War. One might even wonder whether those authorial interventions in *G.* were in reality questions Lukács himself had demanded of Berger, questions that prodded and helped shape up B.'s novelistic ambitions. (Telling a story and telling a story of the novel's story should be, Lukács insists, part and parcel of the same writer's craft.) For Lukács, the historian and philosopher of the novel, the novel-form is 'the prose of life', the 'mirror-image of a world gone out of joint'.

Since the ancient Greeks, Lukács says, there have been several great paradigmatic forms of world literature. First we had tragedy, outlining the cruel and senseless arbitrariness of human destiny, all of which, according to Lukács, gave rise to tragic problems within the genre itself: a monological and solitary dialogue sometimes swamps the clarity and definition of the words exchanged. In the wake of tragedy, though, came the epic, which gives form to 'the extensive totality of life, drama to the intensive totality of essence'. The problem here is that the epic tries to do too much; it ends up creating an art that's airless and essentially empirical, a literary form that is 'closed within itself'.

The epic, Lukács says, can never 'transcend the breadth and depth, the rounded, sensual, richly ordered nature of life as historically given'. Needless to say, this produces artistic riches for understanding specific epochs. But epic cannot be properly utopian, can't break free of its historical moorings, without falling back into anachronism, without falling back into either the lyrical or the dramatic. True, this 'falling back' produces its own 'marvelous elegiac lyricism'; yet neither the dramatic nor the epic can ever put 'real life into a content that transcends being'.

Enter, then, the *novel*, which for Lukács is the privileged literary device whose content does not reside within 'the finished form'. In fact the novel's whole being – its normative being – lies precisely in its *becoming*. Here the protean form of the novel comes into its own: its diversity means that its inner life can never be as pure and as organic as the epic, its totality never a closed totality. But this incompleteness is its strength. The novel's power, Lukács says, lies in its ability to represent history's changing characters and events; as a literary genre it can more effectively reflect and respond to epochal historico-philosophical moments. In its utopian guise it can also transcend those moments, and help invent new ones. 'The inner form of the novel', says Lukács, almost of *G.*,

> has been understood as the process of the problematic individual's journeying towards himself, the road from dull captivity within a merely present reality – a reality that is heterogeneous in itself and meaningless to the individual – towards clear self-recognition.

The conflict within the novel of what is and what ought to be cannot and should not be abolished. Instead, says Lukács, a writer struggles for some kind of conciliation, struggles to give scope to the novel's normative content, to open the way towards an honest recognition of ourselves – and to provide a glimpse, at least, of a potential resolution of life's great tensions. In *G.* we glimpse Berger, the novelist, grappling with the great tensions of the modern tradition, tensions Berger somehow incarnated in himself: the schism between the liberated artist and the condemned masses, between the self and society, between individuality and group history, between sensuality and technological progress, between belonging somewhere and feeling at home everywhere. In the latter sense, *G.* is a philosophical novel *par excellence*, philosophical after Novalis' famous definition: 'Philosophy', the German poet said, 'is really homesickness: it's the urge to be at home everywhere.'

The declaration spoke as much to Lukács as it continues to speak to Berger.[3] For Lukács, just as for Berger, philosophy, as a form of life and life form that supplies the content of literary creation, 'is always a symptom of the rift between "inside" and "outside", a sign of the essential difference between the self and the world, the incongruence of soul and deed.' The duality between the individual and the collective, between self-affirmation and historical contingency, between 'inside' and 'outside', is the central rift pervading *G.*, and it expresses itself most vividly in Berger's dialogue between *sex* and the *crowd*.

When Umberto recalls later in life a terrifying childhood encounter with a revolting crowd, he muses:

> Such a crowd is a solemn test of a man. It assembles as a witness to its common fate – within which personal differentiations have become unimportant . . . It has assembled to demand the impossible. Its need is to overthrow the order which has defined and distinguished between the possible and the impossible . . . In face of such a crowd there are only two ways in which a man, who is not already of it, can react. Either he sees in it the promise of mankind or else he fears it absolutely.

In the crowd, Umberto suggests, the self is overwhelmed by the uncontrollable weight of the collective: individual identity, personal differences and character quirks are all unimportant when one gives oneself over to the crowd. One hands over something intimate inside oneself, one loses something, Umberto thinks, when one joins in the crowd. One hands it over to a giant entity assembled to demand the impossible, and the discrepancy between its demands and the impossibility of ever meeting those demands inevitably leads to violence. Inevitably, too, the crowd is mad, mad as hell and raving mad. Thus the promise of mankind, says Umberto, is not easy to see in a crowd: every particular face, every set of eyes, congeals into a singular abstraction. A single pair of eyes, met in the crowd, is enough to reveal the extent of vacant possibility, of palpable impossibility. One is justified, Umberto concludes, in fearing the crowd, fearing its febrile fate.

The orgasm, on the other hand, is seemingly the antithesis of the crowd, of remoteness, of abstraction: it is an act of individual immediacy, of *presentness*, of pure Being, a shared moment but a solo flight of *hereness*. The only poem to be written about sex, says Berger in *G.*, is 'here, here, here, here – now'.[4] But even then, even writing something specific about sex, even writing it well and writing it *now*, somehow diminishes the experience. At those moments, author B. admits, 'I begin to doubt the value of poems about sex.' In sex, says B., writing adequately about this inadequacy of writing about sex, the quality of 'firstness' is continually felt, continually recreated within each sexual encounter, each sexual arousal. At the briefest moments, at the moment of orgasm, this total experience isn't only a physical and nervous reflex; imagin-ation is also deployed – memory, dreams, language – and it takes another person, the desired person, to express life itself, to express yourself, through another, in a strange equation: 'sexual experience = I + life'.[5]

Hence that dramatic tension, that central fault-line structuring *G.*, structuring Berger himself: how to represent that 'I + life'? Is primal human experience solo or social? Is the meaning of life a sexual or a revolutionary process? Is it a spontaneous eruption or a rationally planned act? Is history made in the crotch or in the crowd? Or, as Berger would more subtly ask, as Herbert Marcuse, Erich Fromm and Wilhelm Reich would all some time ask: where can you find the contact zones, the points and body parts of potential overlap, the moment when the sexual climax becomes a revolutionary climax?

In the end it is evident that B. creates the character of Umberto to test out John Berger's own concept of the crowd in history, John

Berger's own idea of the revolutionary potential of the collective, of romantic revolution (in the strict, first sense of the term). Berger believes a dialectical reconciliation is possible and necessary, though in *G.* he's playful and modest about stating it so plainly. *G.*, however, found infantile arousal holding the hands of the Roman girl in the crowd. It was the context as well as the person that animated the sexual drama, the strangeness of its coming together. The titillation was at once internal and external, *intensive* and *extensive*, as Spinoza might have said: the person and the crowd are made of the same *substance*. In *G.*, like in other books to follow, Berger gropes – gropes conceptually, experientially – for an ideal of the individual (man and woman) within a common praxis: he's groping for what Sartre labelled a 'constituted dialectic' of history.

In the 'constituted dialectic', Sartre says, 'the individual cannot achieve the common objective on their own, but they can conceive it, signify it, and, through it, signify the reorganization of the group . . . Individuals integrate themselves into the group and the group has its practical limit in the individual.'[6] Berger puts it similarly, though more romantically, in *G.*:

> The crowd sees the city around them with different eyes. They have stopped the factories producing, forced the shops to shut, halted the traffic, occupied the streets. It is they who have built the city and they who maintain it. They are discovering their own creativity. In their regular lives they only modify presented circumstances; here, filling the streets and sweeping all before them they oppose their very existence to circumstances. They are rejecting all that they habitually, and despite themselves, accept: Once again they demand together what none can ask alone: Why should *I* be compelled to sell my life bit by bit so as not to die? (Emphasis added: Suddenly, the crowd becomes vital for the I's efficacy, for its self-development.)

The most compelling passages on crowds in *G.* became actual reenactments of Berger's theoretical essay 'The Nature of Mass Demonstrations', first published in *New Society* when crowds of young men and women piled onto Europe and America's streets in the spring of 1968.[7] In this discussion Berger hints at his research on the 1898 Milan uprising, when the cavalry charged the crowd and butchered 100 workers, wounding many hundreds more. He is convinced that crowds of people in demonstrations can be distinguished from crowds in riots or even in revolutionary uprisings. The aim of a crowd in a demonstration is essentially *symbolic*: they are rehearsals for revolution, not strategic rehearsals, or tactical ones, but 'rehearsals of revolutionary awareness'.

A mass demonstration, Berger thinks, is a spontaneous event; yet no matter how much it is spontaneous, it is equally something *created by individuals*. People literally come together to create a function, to protest, to demand things; they're not responding to a function like a crowd of shoppers. The crowd at a demonstration acts rather than reacts; or, if they react, it's only to react to what they've already done, to how their actions have been received by the powers that be. In any mass demo, the demonstrating crowd 'simultaneously *extends* and *gives body* to an abstraction'. (This is why Berger could never agree with Umberto.) Crowds here dramatize the power they still lack. 'The historical role of demonstrations is to show the injustice, cruelty, irrationality of the existing state authority. Demonstrations are protests of innocence.' The crowd at a mass demonstration expresses political ambitions before the political means necessary to realize them are created. The revolutionary in the crowd has to learn how to wait, how to symbolically rehearse, how to translate their inner force into an external common and transformative praxis; one has to test out oneself in the collective and strategic drama of the historical performance itself.[8]

We know, 40 years on, that the real climax of *G.* didn't come in the novel at all. Its real climax came later, at the awards ceremony at London's Café Royal in November 1972, when Berger sublimated the considerable sexual energy of G. into political denunciation, laying into Britain's literary establishment, tearing into them as he'd torn into Britain's art establishment in *Ways of Seeing*. 'Since you have awarded me this prize', he said that night,

> you may like to know, briefly, what it means to me. The competitiveness of prizes I find distasteful. And in the case of this prize, the publication of a shortlist, the deliberately publicized suspense, the speculation of the writers concerned as though they were horses, the whole emphasis on winners and losers is false and out of place in the context of literature.

The explosiveness of Berger's smouldering volcano, his anti-imperialist Marxist allegiances, climaxed when he suggested that the Booker McConnell foundation, whose name the prize bears, was an agent of English imperialism. It is perhaps not too hard to imagine the reaction of certain onlookers that night, how they felt hearing and seeing Berger onstage; we have only to turn towards the end of *G.*, when our anti-hero takes the Slovene peasant Nusa to the swanky charity ball. G. wanted to express his revulsion, his defiance of the smart cocktail-drinking bourgeois set; he wanted his defiance to be persistent, to be devious and cumulative, just like Berger wanted. And so there we have it, that night, Berger reenacting G.'s snub, his public denunciation: like G. at the charity ball, arm in arm with the Slav village lass, each moment of Berger's speech was a moment of tension and triumph.

'The reason why the novel is so important', voiced Berger in his Booker Prize speech (see *The Guardian*, 24 November 1972), apparently goaded on by Lukács,

> is that it asks questions which no other literary form can ask: questions about the individual working on his own destiny . . .

The novelist is concerned with the interaction between individual and historical destiny. The historical destiny of our time is becoming clear. The oppressed are breaking through the wall of silence which was built into their minds by their oppressors.

Yet one does not have to be a novelist seeking subtle connections in history

to trace the five thousand pounds of this prize back to the economic activities from which they came. Booker McConnell have had extensive trading activities in the Caribbean for over 130 years. The modern poverty of the Caribbean is the direct result of this and similar exploitation. One of the consequences of this Caribbean poverty is that hundreds of thousands of West Indians have been forced to come to Britain as migrant workers.

That was why Berger was sharing the prize money with the London-based Black Panther movement, 'who are fighting to put an end to their exploitation'. The other half would finance a project about migrant workers, which would eventually materialize as *A Seventh Man* and spill over into his trilogy *Into their Labours*. 'The sharing of the prize', Berger said that infamous night, 'signifies that our aims are the same. By the recognition a great deal is clarified. And clarity is more important than money.'

With *G.* John Berger had become a novelist, a modern novelist: he had found a voice, experimented with a new, innovative style, made amends for past journeyman shortcomings, and given the English novel an art-house Continental twist. He had created his great Cubist moment, a moment that could only ever be a moment: by its very success, by its own dialectical act of progression, by the inner contradictions it had tried to synthesize, *G.* had to devour itself, had to negate itself, had to bite its own tail, get trampled by the crowd. Now the accusation Berger made of Picasso in *The*

Success and Failure of Picasso rang true for Berger himself: Berger's avant-gardism, the genius of his prize-winning *G.*, the purity of his creation, its lined precision, had propelled Berger so far ahead of the game that it separated him from messy reality outside, leaving him stranded, lone, an individual towering artist, just like Picasso. Thus the *Success and Failure of G.*

To move on, to go forward, Berger had to go back, back to something (and somewhere) more pre-modern, to a scene more traditional, full of everyday people. It is almost as if with *G.* he had cut his own umbilical moorings, and now, after becoming a free-floating European intellectual, a modern novelist, he needed to re-centre himself again, had to somehow un-*G.* himself. It is almost as if Berger now, somehow, had to return to a source, had to tell stories, even to defy Lukács, negate Musil, to find active heroes and people *with* qualities.

G. didn't have those blemishes, those holes for light and air, those torn-up defects, the wonderful humility and approachable humanity that would be so reminiscent of subsequent Berger books. And while plenty of semen flowed, there wasn't any shit in *G.*, there wasn't any muck: *G.* gave us a sexual reality devoid of earthly sensuous reality, a literature of purity not putrefaction; the *clin d'œil* 'Geneva–Paris–Bonnieux' may have been Joycean, but there wasn't the 'offal with flecks of the divine' that Berger acknowledged in *Ulysses*.

Meanwhile the power of *G.*'s lines, lines Janos Lavin had revelled in, were lines that expressed an urban face, intellectual lines, travelled lines, experienced and strained, earned through reading books, furrowed by hours and hours of dutiful study, done by the midnight oil. They were lines of pale not ruddy flesh, not florid skin, not a face tanned and made colourful in the open air, in fresh air, shaped though manual labour, with calloused hands. ('No soft hands', exclaimed Proudhon to his bookish socialist peers, 'only those with calluses!') To un-*G.* himself, then,

Berger had to change clothes, had to put away his loafers and don peasant boots, Van Gogh's boots. He had to learn not how to travel further, as G. desired, but how to go lower: he had, in short, to learn how to wallow in pig earth.

3

Van Gogh's Boots

Van Gogh's boots shovel shit and plough the pig earth. Those there boots are peasant boots, working boots, boots that belong. And they enter into their labours.

> From the dark opening of the worn insides, the toilsome tread of the worker stares forth. In the stiffly rugged heaviness of the shoes there is the accumulated tenacity of a slow trudge through the far-spreading and ever-uniform furrows of the field swept by a raw wind. On the leather lie the dampness and richness of the soil. Under the soles slides the loneliness of the field-path as evening falls. In the shoes vibrates the silent call of the earth, its quiet gift of the ripening grain and its unexplained self-refusal in the fallow desolation of the wintry field.

So speaks the eloquent voice of German philosopher Martin Heidegger, in his celebrated essay 'The Origin of the Work of Art' (1935) on Van Gogh's even more celebrated painting from 1886. Those leather boots, those peasant's boots, are old and tatty yet they reveal, Heidegger thinks, something fundamental about our Being-in-the-world, express a primal truth about life and our relationship with nature, especially with working nature, with the nature of productive work.

Van Gogh's boots, says Heidegger, convey 'the equipmental being of equipment'. 'This equipment,' he adds, 'is pervaded by uncomplaining anxiety about the certainty of bread . . . The equipment belongs to the earth, and it is protected in the world.' Those there boots Van Gogh painted, actually in his Paris workshop far away from any field, somehow internalize the very essence of rural misery, of backbreaking brutality, of authentic graft in its most primitive and marginal form, in its purest and most honest state.

In the late 1960s the American art critic Meyer Schapiro claimed, contra Heidegger, that those there boots belonged to no peasant, to no peasant woman (as Heidegger thought): they were, in fact, Van Gogh's own boots, an artist's boots; country boots for sure, caked in mud and beat up through much stomping over fields and down rough lanes (Van Gogh was a passionate walker); yet they were boots worn by a man of the town and the city, like Berger trying to un-*G.* himself, reacting against the modern world's neurosis of hygiene, against a fabricated and false purity bereft of sensuous reality. 'Heidegger ignores what those shoes meant to the painter Van Gogh himself', Schapiro says. 'They're seen as if endowed with feelings and reverie about himself. In isolating his old, worn shoes on a canvas, he turns them to the spectator; he makes of them a piece from a self-portrait . . . a memorable piece of his own life.' In reality, the true Being of those boots, says Schapiro, turns out to be the true Being of 'the artist's presence in his work'.

Entering into their labours, accordingly, means entering into Berger's boots, trudging with him over lonely *alpage* as snow falls, traipsing through fields swept by a raw wind. In those there boots we'll encounter alpine outcasts recast in the lively light of Berger's own imagination, dead souls and independent women, *colporteuses* who have had axes buried in their skulls yet who live on in weird afterlives; we will stumble upon real peasants who worked themselves into early graves, or discover others who did themselves in because they could no longer find work.

'I am not a peasant', Berger qualifies at the beginning of *Pig Earth* (1979), the opening salvo of his trilogy *Into Their Labours* examining 'the historical elimination' of the peasantry. Now, seven years on from *G.*, Berger feels 'an explanation' befits any would-be reader, the more so for anybody who'd feted his Booker Prize-winning effort. 'I am a writer: my writing is both a link and a barrier . . . Whatever the motives, political or personal, which have led me to undertake to write something, the writing becomes, as soon as I begin, a struggle to give meaning to experience.'

'Experience' is now the stuff Berger's stories are made of. 'Experience' isn't synonymous with thinking; it's more than the strictly cerebral, more than something that comes from the head. It flows through the senses, emanates from the heart, goes right to the brain and ends up deep down in the soul. It is corporeal and bodily, spontaneous and fluid – not rational and linear, not something that correlates with numbers, not something that can be proven. How to give meaning to such a fuzzy reality as 'experience'? How to give meaning to it with words? 'The act of approaching a given moment of experience', Berger says, 'involves both scrutiny (closeness) and the capacity to connect (distance).' As the act of writing unfolds, as it grapples with its subject-matter – and writing is nothing without subject-matter, having 'no territory of its own' – as the writer closes in and backs off, the nearness to experience increases. As this movement of writing repeats itself, repeats and repeats, 'its intimacy with the experience increases. Finally, if one is fortunate, meaning is the fruit of this intimacy.'[1]

On the one hand *Pig Earth* marks Berger's reliance on a more traditional narrative form, on straight storytelling; on the other *Pig Earth* is just as innovative as *G.*, just as experimental and daring and groundbreaking in its artistic application. (*Pig Earth* reads like a verbal equivalent of Malevich's Cubo-Futurist peasant painting *Morning in the Village after Snowstorm* (1912); both are full of the same modernist distortions, the same time-space compressions; both hover constantly between abstraction and representation, between imagination and perception.) There are seven short stories in *Pig Earth*, otherworldly in their depictions of all-too-earthly alpine life. Poems cue each tale and, like *G.*, the author is tormented by his need to intervene, to qualify his drama, to explain himself. Berger somehow *has* to come clean about his own stakes, about what he is up to here, about how things have changed, about what partisan subjectivity means in his quest for impartial objectivity.

Hence two non-fiction essays bookend the fictionalized stories: the first, 'An Explanation', is a methodological meditation, an invitation to the reader to enter into the writer's head, to look over his shoulder, to watch him scribbling away at his writing desk, to discreetly follow him around the village talking to locals; the second, a 'Historical Afterword', is a political and economic delineation of peasants in world history. As a creative whole *Pig Earth* is a curious mix of genres and styles, of the poetic and subtly imaginative – epitomized by the wonderfully humane 'The Three Lives of Lucie Cabrol' – and the rhetorical and assertive, wherein Berger aggressively lays into those forces that continue to annihilate peasant existence.

Why peasants? Berger made it clear, post-*G.*, that he wanted to do something on migrant labour, something ethnographic, something close-up, something that would redouble his allegiance with the oppressed, consolidate his anti-capitalist, anti-imperialist yearnings. He had made it clear, too, that he wanted to see not only where migrants ended up, where they would labour as seventh men, but also where they had set off from and what they had left behind, what they had forsaken. Berger surprised many – friends and enemies alike – when his creative and political ambitions got personalized, when they prompted a decision not to camp out near peasants, not to study them for a few months as any anthropologist might, but to actually live among them, to set up his home within their diminishing throng.

So from Geneva to Quincy he came, leaving Lukács, Musil and his own history of the novel behind, filing them away on the other side of the Salève – the metropolitan side. Berger would likewise finish with partner Anya Bostock, whose high modernist, polyglot gifts had been so influential in Berger's career as a critic and novelist. Berger and Bostock had both been engaged in the same adventure, an adventure that after *G.* would give rise to a new chapter, to a different mode of expression, and ultimately to a different woman. (Perhaps Anya was incredulous of Berger's passionate embrace of peasants?) Berger and his new partner Beverly Bancroft, a publisher working for Penguin in London whom Berger had encountered at the 1972 Frankfurt Book Fair when she had been promoting *Ways of Seeing*, would experiment not only in literature but also in life, in rural mountain life, in really going native.

In living among peasants he and Beverly would henceforth share a disappearing experience, share peasant habitat and habits, share with them the same duties of fatherhood and motherhood, and comparable standards of comfort (and discomfort); they would participate in village life, in village ceremonies, in births and marriages, in sicknesses and deaths. Yet because they were not born in the village both would remain, by the standards of a peasant, forever outsiders, forever strangers who have chosen to live here, strangers who can leave at any time.[2] That choice is already a mark of privilege. A peasant has no such choice, no such privilege. Instead they are condemned to a place.

'It is very rare for a peasant to remain a peasant and be able to move', Berger explains in *Pig Earth*. 'He has no choice of locality. Therefore it is logical that he treats where he is born as the centre of his world.' The stranger can win acceptance, can earn it through making a contribution to peasant ways, likely a modest contribution; they can win acceptance if they don't impose themselves on the life of the village, if their interests do not come into conflict with villagers' interests.

Thus in the land of peasants, the then 50-year-old global intellectual became a clumsy little boy again, a novice who had to re-learn his craft, had to do it in another tongue, had to play the role of double agent. 'Thus', Berger says, 'in our double role as novices and independent witnesses, a certain reciprocity has been established. Often the lesson given to me as a novice was also a request for the recognition and comment of myself as witness. "Have you ever met T . . . No? Then come. I'll introduce you. And perhaps one day you'll write a story with him in it."'[3]

Peasants are not agricultural labourers: their livelihood does not depend on wages. They are small-scale producers who, with the

With peasants after haymaking.

help of limited equipment and with the labour of their families, produce food for themselves and for others. They labour for their own subsistence under obligations imposed upon them: namely the permanent handicap of having a 'surplus' taken from them. To survive – and the peasant is above all else a being committed to survival – they must meet the basic needs of their families while fulfilling their obligations to political and economic power. And always and everywhere the peasant fulfils those latter obligations *before* fulfilling their own needs.

But a peasant's exploitation is not like that of a politically unconscious proletarian: a peasant's economic relation to the rest of society is transparent. The wage-labourer may be unaware of the surplus they create for their employer. In advanced capitalist society, the wage-relation is obfuscated by a myriad of factors, by a detailed division of labour that hacks up different aspects of any production process, a staggeringly complicated separation between where things get produced and where they eventually get distributed and exchanged at markets. (Marx called this obfuscation 'fetishism', the idea that the 'thing-form' of the commodity throws a veil over the activities and exploitation occurring at its point of production.)

Peasants, however, know perfectly well they are being ripped off. There is no veil or division of labour at play because a peasant is connected to everything they do, to every act of labour they carry out. Invariably the peasant struggle is a struggle between themselves and the 'natural' hazards of agriculture: bad seasons and droughts, pests and storms, crop failures and animal or plant diseases. Moreover the peasant has historically been susceptible to wars and pillaging, and to genocide, previously under state-managed socialism, nowadays under corporate-inspired agri-capitalism.

In the late 1970s, when Berger embarked upon *Pig Earth*, the majority of people in the world lived in the countryside and toiled as peasants. Not so anymore. Now the balance has tilted: the majority of the world's population lives in cities, in massively expanding mega-cities, the majority of which are in the developing world, in Asia, Africa and in Latin America. These new urban populations comprise ex-peasants, people forcibly displaced from their land, thrown off it by modernization schemes, by 'efficiency' drives of capitalist agriculture, by neoliberal trade policies, by International Monetary Fund (IMF) 'structural adjustment' quackery, by land tenure transformations, by anything that can get rid of the peasant, wipe them out, out of sight and out of mind, anything that can promote mono-crop production and shareholder profitability. 'Many of these ex-peasants', Berger warned in 1979,

> make for the cities where they form a million-fold mass such as has never existed before, a mass of static vagrants, a mass of unemployed attendants: attendants in the sense that they wait in the shanty towns, cut off from the past, excluded from the benefits of progress, abandoned by tradition, serving nothing.

Everything he writes about peasants, Berger says, every story he pens about their experience, about their ways of life, about their traditions, about their black humour, their loose tittle-tattle, their bitter feuds, isn't done because of *nostalgia*, isn't done because he wants to idealize their existence, their lifestyle, their peasant boots. In a just world, Berger knows that such a class would no longer exist. And yet, at the same time, to dismiss their experience as simply 'belonging only to the past, as having no relevance to modern life, to imagine that the thousands of years of peasant culture have no heritage for the future', is, he says, 'to deny the value of too much history and too many lives'.[4]

'Meanwhile' – and this 'meanwhile' says bundles about Berger's *altermondialiste* politics today –

if one looks at the unlikely future course of world history, envisaging either the further extension and consolidation of corporate capitalism in all its brutalism, or a prolonged, uneven struggle against it, a struggle whose victory is not certain, the peasant experience of survival may be better adapted to this long and harsh perspective than the continually reformed, disappointed, impatient progressive hope of an ultimate victory.[5]

Seen in this light, peasant conservatism has nothing in common with ruling class conservatism: it has no privilege to defend. Instead it is 'a conservatism not of power but of meaning', a 'depository of meaning', Berger calls it, preserved by generations of people threatened with continual change as well as progressive annihilation.

What is more, the peasant suspicion of 'progress', Berger thinks, 'as it has finally been imposed by the global history of corporate capitalism and by the power of this history even over those seeking an alternative to it, is not entirely misplaced or groundless'. (One might wonder, too, whether the current model of corporate agribusiness really represents 'progress' in the quality and sustainability of our food system. Having land on which to grow food, even a modest smallholding, is still one of the best mechanisms for coping with the vagaries of global food markets.)

In *The Communist Manifesto* (1848) Marx was culpable of two things: he *over*estimated the developmental capacity of the capitalist mode of production and *under*estimated the resilience of the peasantry. He saw the peasantry as inhibiting the passage *through* capitalism; the proletarianization of the peasantry, transformed into the ranks of an industrial working class, was, for Marx, a necessary prerequisite for socialism. The destruction of self-sufficiency, the centralization of the productive forces and the rise of big urban areas – in which physical proximity would create collective solidarity – was the major reason Marx praised the long and rapid march of the bourgeoisie, praised them as playing the 'most revolutionary part'. 'In place of the old local and national seclusion and self-sufficiency,' he says,

> we have intercourse in every direction . . . In place of the old wants, satisfied by the productions of the country, we find new wants, requiring for their satisfaction the products of distant lands and climes . . . The bourgeoisie has subjected the country to the rule of the towns. It has created enormous cities, has greatly increased the urban population as compared with the rural, and has thus rescued a considerable part of the population from the idiocy of rural life.

With the noblest of motives, Marx extols the modernizing 'virtues' of bourgeois capitalism for melting things into air, for revealing to the labouring classes, 'with sober senses', the real conditions of their life and their relations with their kind. But has this 'progress' meant more personal and social fulfilment or has it not brought about greater mass manipulation? Has the economic integration of the globe, this long and supposedly temporary passage through capitalism, brought greater peace or has it perpetuated genocide? How long must it be before the capitalist integument is finally blown asunder by the hypertrophic development of the productive forces? Berger is adamant that the universalization of capitalism, the dissemination of its knowledge-base, of its business 'ethics', of its legalized fraud and mass finagling, of its accumulation by dispossession, 'is not leading unequivocally to greater democracy but rather to its contrary'.

All told, the isolation of the peasantry, their self-sufficiency, their family-run smallholdings, their hostility to change, their lack of a division of labour, of scientific application, of extended social relations, meant, for Marx, only an incapacity to enforce its class interests in its own name. The peasantry, he says in *The Eighteenth Brumaire* (1846), describing the French peasantry of his day, is nothing other than a great homologous mass of insert objects coexisting with one another 'much as potatoes in a sack form a sack of potatoes'. As such, the peasantry, Marx declares, 'cannot represent themselves, they must be represented'.[6]

Pig Earth concerns itself precisely with this thorny question of *representation*, of how to *represent the peasantry* given that they cannot represent themselves. How can a writer who is not a peasant *represent the meaning of peasant experience*? The act of representation, of speaking on behalf of the peasantry, of recounting their stories, vividly yet honestly, imaginatively yet realistically, brings us back to the same dilemma Van Gogh confronted with those peasant boots: how does an artist portray the real in all its reality? For any experimental artist or writer – who, remember, is not a mere 'reporter' of reality, a simple conveyor of 'facts' – through what medium can a truth be best revealed, be best invented, created even? Otherwise put: how can reality be made more real for the reader, real enough for them to enter the experience, enter body and mind?

Berger has tackled this theme of representing those who cannot represent themselves from a number of different angles, using different media. He has tried it with Jean Mohr, via photo-documentary realism, mobilizing textual commentary alongside graphic pictures of peasants in action and at rest; he has also deployed more conventional literary 'realism', straight essays and simple narratives in which trenchant criticism frequently waxes poetical. He has likewise pushed this realist form further, often letting rip imaginatively, rendering peasant experience more real by making it more magically real (for example, 'The Three Lives of Lucie Cabrol'). The fluidity and beauty (and accessibility) of this latter approach is worlds removed from academic 'peasant studies', where rural sociologists, historians and anthropologists tend to place subjective experience within its grander objective structure; actual peasant destinies thereby get reduced to abstract meta-narrative realities, to the remote contingency of history rather than the intimate fragility of individuality.

A month or so after *Pig Earth* was released, Berger and Mike Dibb (from 'Ways of Seeing') came together again to bring Berger's loving stories alive for television, creating a 50-minute documentary for the BBC's *Omnibus* series. The film is noteworthy for a number of reasons, not least because it gave viewers an early glimpse of the photographs that would eventually fill *Another Way of Telling* (1982). *Pig Earth*, the book, is not illustrated; 'I am very sorry, Jean', is how Jean Mohr recalled Berger's conversation,

> but I shall have to do without your photos this time. I'm not writing a documentary book, and the reader will have to see my characters in the imagination and shape them accordingly. In any case, you can imagine the effect on my neighbours if they were to recognize themselves – it doesn't bear thinking about!

With Mike Dibb, filming 'Pig Earth'.

In front of camera, 'Pig Earth'.

And yet in 'Pig Earth', the documentary, Mohr's photos play a star visual role. Berger is there once more, in front of the camera, eyeballing his audience as he did in 'Ways of Seeing', seducing the viewer; a sequence of his colleague's photos line the wall behind him. Fields of peasants now become fields of memory. The world these photos reveal, frozen, Berger says, becomes intractable. Feeling permeates the information they contain. Appearances become the language of a lived life. A photo, says Berger, is a moment from the past, a reminder that everything passes. Photographs are the opposite of films, he says. Before a photograph you search for *what was there*. In cinema you wait for what is to come next. 'One day', he continues, stood beside a group of images of Gaston, a Mieussy woodcutter, 'Gaston's wife stopped me in the village and said: "I'd like to ask you a favour. Would you ask your friend to take a photo of my husband? I don't have one, and if he's killed in the forest I won't have a picture to remember him by."'

Gaston, unlike most woodcutters, works alone. He knows this is more dangerous than working in a team. But he has a passion for forests and enjoys them in solitude. He also works too fast for a lot of other woodcutters. 'You can take some pictures', he tells Mohr, 'on condition that they show what the *work* is like.' Dibb's moving camera zooms into Mohr's fixed camera, into the latter's photograph, the latter who's trying to frame an image *on behalf of the photographed*. A 40-something Gaston, covered in wood chippings and sawdust, looks up at a giant tree, surveying heaven as his chainsaw cuts a deep wedge into its mighty trunk. Another sequence shows the tree being felled, bit by bit, eventually toppling within 20 centimetres of where Gaston planned it: 'That's the kind of photo I've dreamed of since I began cutting down trees', he says. Then, finally, the portrait his wife wanted: a raw, ruggedly handsome face, tanned with only a few grey hairs; a brow furrowed with concentration, an expression of brave torment, of doubt, of supplication. 'There are no trees in it', Berger says, 'but the expression on his face is easier to understand if one knows something about the forest.'

There are a lot of photographs of Marcel, too, the richest peasant in the village, Marcel *le roi*, with his 50 cows. We see Marcel at work on the *alpage*, milking his herd, eating in his shack chalet, the chalet we've already visited near Sommand; elsewhere he is lying down on a hillside meadow next to his grandson; then there's a long shot of him walking on a slope with all his cows, his grandson, his dog and goats, which was the picture he liked best. 'That's very good! It's all there', all the things that gave Marcel the most pleasure in life: his cows, his grandson and his dog, out in the open air, on the mountainside, in bright sunshine.

One Sunday, Berger recounts, early morning, Marcel knocks at Berger's door, clean-shaven, hair combed, wearing a freshly ironed shirt. Below, because Sunday is still a working day, he's wearing old trousers and boots covered in cowshit. 'Is Jean there?' Marcel demands hurriedly. 'The moment has come', he says, 'to take my bust.' Down to there, down to his waist, he indicates with his hand.

And so there Marcel stood, in the middle of the Bergers' kitchen, composing himself before Mohr's camera, standing proudly with arm on hip. It was the image *he was giving*, an image of a simple peasant, the one he'd chosen of himself – the image, Berger muses, that would most resemble him on his deathbed, laid out before the neighbours for all to see. 'And now', Marcel beams, inspecting the final print of Mohr's photograph, 'my great-grandchildren will know what sort of man I was.'

There's another peasant called Marcel in *Pig Earth*, a Marcel who clings onto the land, a Marcel who knows that working 45 hours a week in a factory is no life for a man, that that leads to ignorance. There are no images of this Marcel so this time we have to invent him in our imagination, recreate him from Berger's short story version, just as he had told Jean Mohr. Yet we've somehow met his type before. He owns a stocky shire horse called Gui-Gui, as strong as an ox, bearing a distinct resemblance to her master. One day Marcel's son, Edouard, buys his father a twelve-year-old tractor: 'I got it cheap', the son announces ebulliently. Edouard and Marcel don't exactly see eye to eye. Edouard is a modern young man who does not want to kill himself like Pops toiling the land, nor does he want to fritter away his life in any factory. So he chooses the life of a travelling salesman, selling soap and other domestic wares on the road and in the open air. His son cheats people, Marcel thinks, he doesn't practice a trade. And that tractor he's bought is useless because Marcel can't drive, doesn't want to drive. Machines make monkey-work productive, Marcel says, and the wealth they create goes to those who own the machines.

'He's boneheaded', Marcel's wife exclaims, denouncing her husband. 'They make sure we know the machines exist', Marcel utters under his breath.

From then onwards working without one is harder. Not having the machine makes the father look old-fashioned to the son, makes the husband look mean to his wife, makes one neighbour look poor to the next. After he has lived a while with not having the machines they offer him a loan to buy a tractor.

What he earns from his milk each year is the price of a tractor. That's why he needs a loan.

But with a tractor he needs all the parts, all the machinery, all the gizmos that come with it, without which the tractor doesn't go. So more loans are required for more machines. Soon the peasant falls deeper and deeper into debt. Eventually he's forced to sell out, to get a job, if he's lucky, in the local factory, providing the local factory hasn't gone bust or gone abroad. Selling out – it's what those city slickers planned all along, those city slickers in *Paris* – Marcel, Berger points out, pronounces the name of the capital with contempt and recognition in that order. (It was in Paris that fellow villager Catherine, an 'independent woman', first heard the word *peasant* used as an insult.) 'The world has left the earth behind it', Marcel says to Edouard. 'And what was on the earth?' demands the angry son. 'Half the men here had to emigrate because there wasn't enough to eat! Half the children died before they grew up! Why don't you admit it!'

Marcel has a vat full of *marc*, dregs of apples which he ferments each year to create *gnôle*, rocket fuel eau-de-vie. The *marc* gives off warmth in the cold air of winter and Marcel shovels it into sacks and hauls it by horse and cart to the village distillery. Peasants drink *gnôle*, use it as antiseptic for themselves and their animals, preserve fruit and herbs in it, cook in it, cook sausages that release dreams because they're salty and spicy and saturated in alcohol. But the authorities tax *gnôle*, treat it almost as though it is illegal moonshine, bootleg liquor. From time to time inspectors tour the villages on the lookout for surplus *gnôle*, *gnôle* beyond the statutory 20 litres, *gnôle* that needs to be taxed. (Everything that brings pleasure to the poor, Marcel laments, *they* tax.)

In the middle of a snowstorm a strange car stops on the bridge. 'The buggers have come back again!' Marcel and other villagers in the distillery call out. Then two men get out, 'wearing city over-coats, spotless green Wellington boots'. They greet the villagers yet nobody greets the inspectors back. 'Marcel's *marc* has yielded one hundred and sixty litres of eau-de-vie at fifty percent', which meant, the oldest inspector says, speaking as if he were explaining to children, 'that he had to pay on eighty six litres the sum of two hundred and six thousand, four hundred francs.'

Later that afternoon Marcel seeks vengeance, seeks justice as the countryside strikes back against the city, against paper money and its paper laws. He stops the inspectors' car at gunpoint, leads them away to a distant hayloft stinking of *gnôle* and piss, and locks them up in the dark with a bunch of shaggy sheep. Meanwhile he dumps their car over a ravine, and for a while lets them feel a rural cold, a rural suffering. Before he releases his prisoners, before the police come to handcuff Marcel, before they eventually sentence him to two years in jail for rebellion against officers of the state, armed robbery and wilful destruction of public property, one inspector begs the peasant to tell how much he's asking for them. 'Is it more than fifty million? I'd say fifty million is the maximum one could expect them to pay for men like us.'

Marcel appears not to hear. How much? they ask again. 'You must understand', the eldest inspector says, 'that we have more experience than you of the value of money.' Then Marcel thrusts his fist into the fleece of the nearest sheep, and spoke almost through the animal: 'The value of money! The value of money!' he cries. 'You are worried', he adds.

I regret to have to tell you that there is a tax on worry! There's also a tax to pay on pain and a tax on shivering. A thousand francs a shiver! If only one of you had stayed warm, it would have saved you money! Have you filled in the form for your pain? You spoke of an ulcer, that's a sharp pain, and the sharper the pain, the higher the tax!

What's regrettable, Marcel knows, is that the inspectors belong to another time, to another world, to linear rather than cyclical time. It is impossible to take revenge on them because they will never understand, never really know what Marcel is trying to avenge, never understand his world, the logic of his actions, his motives, his concept of justice. Nor will the judge or jury. Theirs is an abstract world, a world of abstract wealth, abstract laws, abstract money, illusions in which everything appears to be a game, a game of role-playing, a game of fictitious assets, of seasons where nobody feels the heat or the cold and where tomatoes can be had all the year round.

The peasant's world, on the other hand, is *immediate*, their value theory is concrete, made up of concrete labour, because they themselves are in the habit of handling and doing everything. They touch it with their own hands, feel it with their own bodies, without mediation, without institutions. The inspectors' and the peasants' worlds never meet. In the world of depersonalized institutions and modern mediated forms of power, it's rare that anybody can confront, face-to-face, one's real enemy, and rarer still that they can pick them up by the lapels and toss them out of the village: twenty-first-century power is too cowardly for that. Marcel knew it but could never quite live with it. The saddest thing of all, he says, right at the end of Berger's 'The Value of Money' story, is that they have taken away his life force: 'the habit of working. I will never again be able to load thirteen tipcarts', he says, 'and take Gui-Gui to the top field.'

Lucie Cabrol is another peasant who knew the value of money, learned it the hard way; but she managed to tap the secret of *their* value theory, too. She crossed the frontier between the two worlds, vacillated back and forth between the two concepts of wealth, did it every week, even while her own kind ostracized her, even while they disinherited her, abandoned her. She knew that money did not have the same value on both sides of the frontier, that there is a cheap side and an expensive side. Lucie is Berger's grittiest peasant survivor, his most famous short-story character, the infamous Cocadrille, the pig earth incarnate, conceived in the mountains and raised in a dung heap like a mushroom, like a girolle mushroom born tiny and which stays tiny all its life, even in its afterlife.[7]

All her life, like a little child, the Cocadrille had disappeared, withdrew her labour, desisted from doing things. Her peasant stubbornness had her stubbornly refuse the peasant predicament. Her family dreaded her, her brothers avoided her; she grew up alone, wizened and diminutive, a wrinkled, cider-apple-faced dwarf who isn't a dwarf. She lived by herself, at first in an isolated mountaintop chalet, ate by herself, hardly speaking to anyone. She stole, raided villagers' gardens, pilfered their eggs; it's said that she even burned down her brothers' *grenier*, his cherished hayloft. So they banished her to a lonely roadmender's house, vacant forever, next to a steep precipice and far enough away from the village to trouble nobody.

Slowly but surely the Cocadrille discovers the frontier town, the magical universe in which participants are like bees against a windowpane: you see the events, the colours, the lights, yet something which you can't see separates you.

Month by month the Cocadrille learnt where she could sell each item in the city, each item which, according to the season, she scavenged from the mountains: wild cherries, lilies of the valley, snails, mushrooms, blueberries, raspberries, wild strawberries, blackberries, *trolles*, juniper berries, cumin, wild rhododendra, mistletoe.

Twice a week for years and years she crosses the *douane* with her contraband, the *colporteuse* from the valley with its 'endless laundry of the damned' to the nether world of boundless riches, of jewellery and make-up, of stockings and idle time, of little foresight and thrift which lures her and which, like her own peasant world, she in equal measure despises. (That world sounds ominously like Geneva.)

The Cocadrille is Berger's most complex peasant spirit and his tenderest peasant tale.[8] With her we become conscious, perhaps for the first time, of what peasants are in danger of becoming, of where they are headed: with the Cocadrille we recognize the impossibility of leaving behind the peasantry, that the passage of time is really a time of brief passage. Berger needs the Cocadrille to show us how, in the mountains, the past is never behind you: it's always to the side.

> You come down from the forest at dusk and a dog is barking in a hamlet. A century ago in the same spot at the same time of day, a dog, when it heard a man coming down through the forest, was barking, and the interval between the two occasions is no more than a pause in the barking.

But just as Berger needs the Cocadrille, it is clear, too, that the Cocadrille needs Berger as her narrator, as somebody who bears witness; she needs 'Jean' to be the only man who talks to her, to 'Lucie', the only man likely to have ever impregnated her, the only man whom Lucie wants to marry, could marry, the only man who understands the same sad sense of loss. And Jean is the only man who really knows Lucie, loves Lucie, who is close enough and distant enough to see her in all her fragile ambiguity, the only person who sees her in her afterlife, who's haunted by Lucie after she is felled by an axe, after the blade of an unknown assailant, there to rob her of her accumulated treasure, has split open her birdlike skull.

'Jean' Berger helps translate Lucie's story. As the narrator he puts it into our own language, lets it be felt and heard and hence shared, universalized. This is a voice that no more speaks of arrogant, swashbuckling Giovanni-wannabes, but whispers an ordinary human madness, an ordinary human yearning, an ordinary – well, sort of ordinary – human death. It is a voice now more vernacular in its traditionalism, more craftsman-like in its intellectualism, more artisanal in its internationalism. In backing away from the cosmopolitan modernism of *G.*, Berger has seemingly turned his back on Lukács. He has edged instead towards Walter Benjamin once again, salvaged what the latter believed a dying art: in embracing peasants, migrant workers, the deep song of places and actual experience that's passed on down the line, invariably orally, by word of mouth, by word of rumour, Berger has reinvented himself as a *storyteller*. He has resuscitated something Benjamin thinks, in his essay 'The Storyteller' (1936), is inalienable, is one of our 'securest possessions' nonetheless in grave danger of slipping away: 'the ability to exchange experiences'.

4

Showing Voice

'Experience which is passed on from mouth to mouth is the source from which all storytellers have drawn. And among those who have written down tales, it is the great ones whose written version differs least from the speech of the many nameless storytellers.'

Walter Benjamin, 'The Storyteller'

The stranger walks across the island sand, walks towards the camera. He is walking tall, sprightly, a little playfully. He is dressed all in black with a grey hat and his suit suggests he is an undertaker from another time, from another century, perhaps a century to come. He's a Death secretary, yet somehow, at the same time, he's the Wedding Guest, too, about to tell a story of life, of real life and love, of a couple close by. We cannot choose but hear. He stops to feed a horse a carrot, a carrot he had in his pocket. He walks into a strange room full of strangers, a waiting room where strangers wait. The plane going to the mainland is late: they must wait. The stranger sits down among them. He is not a ghost, because the living are immediately aware of his presence. They fidget, they seem distant from him, and him from them. Their dress is different. Nonetheless, 'the storyteller', Benjamin says, 'takes what he tells from experience – his own or that reported by others. And he in turn makes it the experience of those who are listening to his tale.'

Prior to his coming, the stranger's arrival was announced, his chronicle a love story foretold. Moments earlier, we saw a still photograph of a valley viewed from a mountaintop, an Alpine valley, the Cocadrille's valley, Marcel's valley, any peasant's valley. We saw a moving image of a cow's backside, her tail swishing from side to side, saw it while a sad trombone played, played us something. We know this playing will play a part in the story. 'So many stories, so many stories here', the stranger suddenly whispers, barely aloud, 'each one waiting to be chosen.' 'Any story', he says, 'is like an open-ticket across the sea, an open-ticket to any place in the world where it happened.' 'It begins', he announces, 'it begins on a bus coming down the mountains . . . "On your left is the city of Verona", says the bus driver over the loudspeaker . . .'.

So unfolds an unlikely Romeo and Juliet romance of Bruno, a peasant trombonist, and Marietta, a dark Italian belle, a story set in the queen of cities: Venice. However unlikely an encounter, we believe in this story nonetheless. And the bewildered listeners in the waiting room begin to believe. They listen and become absorbed. Only viewers of Timothy Neat's 1989 film *Play Me Something*, after Berger's short story, only viewers outside the Hebridean waiting room, can see the real-life images (Jean Mohr's) of Bruno and Marietta, with his black beard and her black eyes. Listeners of the story are compelled to hear only Berger's voice, his showing voice; listeners must create in their own heads what we viewers can see on film.

For Berger is himself the stranger, the dark-suited stranger. Berger the writer is playing at playing Berger the storyteller. Like Lestov was for Benjamin, he is at home in distant places as well as in distant times. *Play Me Something* is a compelling indie film about a compelling indie story from *Once in Europa* (a collection of Berger love stories, the second volume of his *Into Their Labours* trilogy, first published in 1989), a story within a story, a film about a storyteller telling a story, a showing voice made visible as well as audible. Yet in a sense we have no real need to go far, no real need even to go to Venice, nor to the Isle of Barra, because this storytelling voice takes us there, takes us across any sea.[1]

What is it that men have and women don't and which is long and hard? the stranger asks, repeating what the bus driver asks in the written story. Tell us! demand the travellers; tell us! demand listeners' faces – they never ask out loud. Military service, Berger says. Everybody laughs and the vaporetto rocks as it approaches the island, rocks in our mind's eye. It costs more to piss here, here near the Doge's Palace, one peasant says, than to drink a whole case back home. We're not from here, the man with the beard says to the woman with the dark eyes. Do you know what's in this box? he asks. She shakes her head. A trombone. It's not true, she cries. Please, please, play something. Not here, he says, not on the boat.

I'd say you work on a farm, she says. How so? Because you smell of cows. If she'd been a man, he thinks, I'd have punched her. But you, you smell of scent. Yes, I work in a chemist's shop. In the waiting room, on a sofa, the man who's a motorcyclist stretches his arm out near a woman who's a hairdresser; she undoes her red hair from a chignon and the locks tumble down across his arm. Do you like dancing? the dark-eyed one wonders. Soon they dance at the festival organized by *L'Unità*, the Communist daily newspaper. What is it like up your mountain? There are rhododendrons and wild goats. How do they vote in your village? For the right, he says. And you? she asks. I vote for anyone who promises to raise the price of milk. That isn't good for the workers, she says. Milk is all we have to sell, he says.

She has small feet, this Marietta, the stranger remarks. Every-thing between a man and a woman is a question of how much you give up of one thing to have another – an exchange. You are bound to be influenced by the property relations of which you are a part, she says tenderly. The Kulaks sided with the bourgeoisie, she says, and the little peasants with the petty bourgeoisie. You are wrong to think only about the price of milk. She comes from a place of water and islands where there is no earth at all, he tells himself. Peasants are disappearing, the future lies elsewhere, she says. I'd like children, he says. You need a wife then, she says. Stay here, and you'll find a wife. I'd cut off my right hand rather than work in a factory, he says. All the men dancing here, she says, work in a factory. Let's dance. Who's milking the cows tonight?

Later, they jump into a gondola. He stands up and it rocks from side to side. Sit down! Sit down! she shrieks, it'll capsize! One hand trails in the water and the other grasps her breast. He enters her. They look at the lights at the Doge's Palace and they see the bell-tower they'd climbed that afternoon. Play for me. Play me something, she asks, and he turns towards the Palace to play on his trombone a melancholic tune. In the darkness, from behind, she touches him as he plays, his shoulder blades, the nape of his neck, his crotch. Stay and I'll find you work, she sighs, come to Mestri, come . . .

At 3 a.m. the coach departs for the journey back to the village. Most of the band wants to sleep. They switch the lights off and the coach again takes to the road towards Verona. The young drummer next to Bruno has one last joke to tell, and the stranger tells it slyly, just as the plane is ready to leave for Glasgow, taking the listeners away from their island. Do you know what hell is? Do you? Hell is where bottles have two holes and women have none.

The stranger gets up, exits, and ambles back across the sand, disappearing across the sea. Towards the kingdom of the story-teller . . .

Storytelling is an artisanal craft, says Walter Benjamin in 'The Storyteller'. And like all artisanal crafts in the modern industrial age, in our age, it is on the point of extinction. This is not merely a 'symptom of decay', Benjamin says, nor even a 'modern' symptom per se; rather, 'it is only a concomitant symptom of the secular productive forces of history, a concomitant that quite gradually removed narrative from the realm of living speech and at the same time is making it possible to see a new beauty in what is vanishing.' The earliest symptom of storytelling's decline, Benjamin thinks, is the rise of the novel. What separates the novel from the story, he says, is the former's essential dependence on the book, on the written word, the dissemination of which was only possible through the development of printing. What gets spoken and what gets written down are no longer the same words.

The story is principally oral, constitutes voices, often public memory ringing out in one's head that gets uttered in speech, that gets remembered, and noted down – if it is noted down – only afterwards. If the story is about somebody, it is told and retold by everyone, preserved down the line because it's somehow retained, remembered collectively into posterity. The birthplace of the novel, conversely, is the solitary individual, alone in their words. The novelist, says Benjamin, the novelist of, say, *G.*, 'has isolated himself'. Writing and reading novels are consequently lonely affairs.

> In this solitude the reader of a novel seizes upon the material more jealously than anyone else. He is ready to make it com - pletely his own, to devour it, as it were. Indeed, he destroys, he swallows up the material as the fire devours logs in the fireplace.

Benjamin's 'The Storyteller' moves in the exact opposite direction to Lukács' *The Theory of the Novel*, just as *Into their Labours* does with respect to *G.* Lukács admires the novel for its breadth and scope of vision, for its apparent universality; Benjamin extols the story for its narrowness and depth, for its rootedness and apparent particularity. 'A great storyteller', he says, 'will always be rooted in the people, primarily in a milieu of craftsmen.' But with the advent of new forms of mass communication and information, and the growth of the press, storytelling began to recede into 'the archaic'.

Yet just as these elements threatened the story, so, too, says Benjamin, did they begin to threaten the novel itself. Capitalism might be creating a 'world literature' (as Marx thought in *The Communist Manifesto*), but the very instruments that do so, for Benjamin, also bring about a crisis of the novel. Our obsession with generating 'information' is culpable. Benjamin quotes Jean Hippolyte de Villemessant, the founder of the French daily *Le Figaro*, as saying: 'To my readers, an attic fire in the Latin Quarter is more important than a revolution in Madrid.'

So it is no longer intelligence coming from afar (or even close by) that counts; it is no longer knowledge more challenging, more ambiguous: instead, it is the freshest triviality that makes the readiest read. The prime requirement of information is to be 'easily understandable in itself'. If storytelling borrows from the miraculous, from the mystical and from the fairy tale, information beds itself down in *what is*, in what is *soundly plausible*. Every morning brings us news of what is happening elsewhere, 'and yet we are poorer in noteworthy stories. This is because no event any longer comes to us without already being shot through with explanation.'

The two forms – information and story – are thus incompatible; one grows at the expense of the other:

> It is half the art of storytelling to keep a story free from explanation as one produces it . . . The most extraordinary things, marvelous things, are related with the greatest accuracy, but the psychological connection of events isn't forced on the reader. It's left up to readers to interpret things the way they understand them, and with this the narrative achieves an amplitude that information lacks.

Pig Earth and *Once in Europa* both attempt to cultivate something of Benjamin's artisanal craft of storytelling. We know already that Berger sees images in his head, that he has invented different ways of seeing; now, though, these images increasingly congeal into stories, into new ways of telling, into new ways of putting the spoken word authentically on the page, without forcing 'the psychological connection of events'. This narrative voice – this storytelling voice – without 'explanation', without being forced, without feeling the need to explain itself – is even more deftly articulated in *Once in Europa* than in *Pig Earth*. You sense in this latest collection of tales that Berger is discovering heightened storytelling powers, that he is letting himself go, releasing his intellectual grip on the literary form in favour of the spoken form, releasing himself as a writer not by reading more but by listening and looking more, especially to what is going on around him in his own backyard.

Perhaps now he is more settled and accustomed to peasant ways in Quincy. Perhaps now he has proven himself to locals, shown how he can learn, how he can adopt and understand their strange ways. He has absorbed their habits and foibles to such a degree that now abstraction and representation have melded into one. A completely new mode of representation has emerged, poetic yet unpretentious, natural yet insightful, a new Berger voice, a more confident and more mature peasant voice, one that sounds more intimate than intellectual, more brawny than brainy. (Perhaps it is no coincidence that often Berger makes a woman his narrative authority, frequently an older woman, a grandmotherly woman.[2])

Occasionally, as in 'Boris is Buying Horses', Berger hints that he is the storyteller himself, that it is he who is directly observing Boris, the strapping shepherd with gigantic shoulders, a Boris who falls for a cute city gal in an affair fated to end badly, a Boris who 'died like one of his sheep, neglected and starving'. 'What he did to his cattle finally happened to him: he died like one of his animals', Berger, the narrator, repeats. 'He is looking at me now', he says, 'with the same expression. I told you once, dead Boris says, that I had enough poems in my head to fill a book, do you remember?

Now you are writing the story of my life. You can do that because it's finished. When I was still alive, what did you do?' 'On the night when Boris died alone, stretched out on the floor with his three black dogs, it seemed to him that his face had been fitted into her breast ever since he first set eyes on her.' 'And when later, she heard news of Boris's death, she abruptly and surprisingly asked whether he was wearing boots when they found him. No, was the reply, he was barefoot.' 'The three black dogs howled all night when he died . . .'.

The tonality of this story, as though written by a sleuth searching for the simplest of truths, of why Boris, a brutish peasant, could bag a married blonde, of how it was possible that Boris who never gave anything away, Boris who would cheat his own grandmother, Boris who never kept his word, could give his house to a girl with soft hands and who smelled of money? All that, written from the perspective of a death foretold, announced from the outset, bespeaks much of the Bergerian 'Death secretary', of a storyteller dressed in black, present not so much to solve a mystery as to preserve it. 'Most, if not all, stories begin with the death of the principal protagonist', Berger reminds us in that aptly named essay, 'The Secretary of Death' (see *The White Bird*). 'We Death secretaries', he says, 'all carry the same sense of duty, the same oblique shame (we have survived, they have departed) and the same obscure pride which belongs to us personally no more than do the stories we tell.'

The essay 'The Secretary of Death' makes for a fascinating read for a number of interrelated reasons. For a start, it reviews Gabriel García Márquez's *Chronicle of a Death Foretold*, a contemporary whom Berger admires more than any other writer; Berger's insightful remarks here are not made as a critic, then, but as a colleague in the art of storytelling, a colleague whose own sense of history is likewise Marxist. Second is how evidently this García Márquez story (from 1981) seems to have influenced 'Boris is

Buying Horses', if one considers the latter's structure and its form of storytelling. As with García Márquez, ditto with Berger: any story drawn from life begins, for the storyteller, with its end; it moves retrospectively, with hindsight, going forwards by going backwards. Any story, says Berger, 'refers insistently to what is over but it refers to it in such a way that, although it is over, it can be retained. This retaining is not so much a question of recollection as of coexistence, the past with the present.'

The other interesting aspect of 'The Secretary of Death' is that in giving us a chronicle of a *Chronicle of a Death Foretold*, Berger is really giving us a Chronicle of a Storyteller Foretold, his own creative destiny laid bare. His distance from the novel as a novel, certainly from the novel as *G.*, is, accordingly, announced: 'The tradition of storytelling of which I am speaking', he says, 'has little to do with that of the *novel.*' With shades of Benjamin (though curiously unreferenced), the chronicle, Berger says,

is public and the novel is private. The chronicle, like the epic poem, retells more memorably what is already generally known; the novel, by contrast, reveals what is secret in a family of private lives. The novelist surreptitiously beckons the reader into the private home and there, their fingers to their lips, they watch together. The chronicler tells the story in the market-place and competes with the clamour of all the other vendors: his occasional triumph is to create a silence around his words.

The novel, says Berger, is written in the future or the conditional tense, and is, necessarily, about *becoming*. (Shades of Lukács this time, though again unreferenced.) Not so with the story, which is announced in the historic present, telling about something that is over yet doing so in order to remember *now*. Stories are about *being*; they are about people and told to people who still believe that life is a story. In any story there is meaning.

'To ask whether this meaning is objective or subjective is', for Berger, 'already to move outside the circle of listeners. To ask what the meaning is is to ask for the unsayable. Nevertheless the faith in meaning promises one thing: meaning has to be shareable. Such stories begin with mortality but they never end in solitude.'

Odile, too, is haunted by death, by the death of a loved one. In fact, her story, told from her own perspective, narrated as she hang-glides across Cluses and over the valley, clinging onto her hang-gliding son, is a tale of love in the time of a factory; or rather it is a chronicle of two love stories foretold, as well as a chronicle of hate, hatred of a factory, of how it kills and what it does to the living. Odile's story, the centrepiece of *Once in Europa*, is a complexly interwoven soliloquy like Molly's in *Ulysses*, something of tremendous emotional depth, a stream of high-flying consciousness punctuated by lots of 'nos', by lots of tragedies, yet always infused by 'yeses', by 'yes I will Yes'. Shifts in paragraphs mark shifts through peasant generations, from childhood to womanhood, from motherhood to grandmotherhood, from land to factory, from factory to branch plant; in the space of 70 pages, Berger has penned – spoken – a sweeping peasant *Bildungsroman*.

Odile is a smart Savoyard farm kid who grows up into a smart everywoman. She somehow mediates between a bygone world of her father's and mother's generation and the new one to come, a new world that is her world but which already seems bankrupt at birth. Odile's family's romance is a Freudian family romance: full of bitter internal squabbles as much as tenderly love, squabbles between siblings, squabbles between fathers and sons, squabbles between mothers and daughters. Such inexorable battles to over - come the private world are dramatized by perpetual struggles to overcome the public world: struggles to stay on the land, struggles to stop the factory encroaching, struggles to stop the factory closing, struggles to resist going to the city, struggles to resist the city itself.

'The men who worked in the factory smelt of sweat', a young Odile remarks before going off on a scholarship to school in Cluses, the valley's biggest town; 'some of them of wine or garlic, and all of them of something dusty and metallic.' The factory's furnaces throb without cease, producing 30,000 tons of ferromanganese every year, retching toxic blue smoke from its chimneys; men work night and day; the factory makes money, provides jobs for locals whose land no longer provides; it provides jobs for non-locals, too, who begin to arrive in droves; it tests out new alloys, makes experiments, and yet 'it is inert, barren, derelict'. Men on the furnaces breathe air that contains 400,000 dust particles per litre, lethal amounts; chimneys spew out 200 tons of fluorine a year; nearby forests are dying, cows and sheep are poisoned; and before long, the factory belongs to a multinational with factories in 21 different countries. 'Papa had been right about the venom', Odile laments from on high.

Michel worked the furnaces, a young village guy with a motor-bike, a communist. One day he takes a teenage Odile for a ride to Chamonix to see Mont Blanc, and onwards through the tunnel to Italy. They eat a picnic lunch above the tree line; Odile has never before breathed such air. 'When the wind was too cold', she says, 'I put my head down against his leather jacket. I tucked my knees under his legs and held on with one hand to his leather belt.' Her backside is sore afterwards, her hands grimy and hair tangled. But she'd been to Italy, and felt proud. And she was a good passenger: she trusted the driver and she'd let herself go. 'We'll do another trip', Michel promises . . . Two months later, Michel loses both legs; not on his motorbike but in a factory accident, two legs burned to smithereens, reduced to charred stumps.

Stepan also worked the furnaces and lived in EUROPA, a factory dormitory beside the river. Stepan came from Russia, spoke Russian, even though he'd settled in Sweden. He started work three days before Michel's accident; for three days they worked side by side. Stepan was very tall and Odile was very young; he had no prospects, may have even been married, but somehow they fell in love. They laugh together, dance together, make music together and later have sex together, once Odile is in EUROPA, once she quits school, once she becomes his concubine. 'He bent down and picked me up', she recalls, 'so my mouth was level with his, and he kissed me. On the nose. I know so little about him, yet with the years of thinking I have learnt a great deal more from the same few facts. Perhaps there are never many facts when you first love somebody.'

Christian, Odile's hang-gliding son, resembles his father, resembles Stepan, despite them never meeting, despite Christian not remembering. Christian was inside her when it happened, at 4:30 a.m. shift time, when the furnace devoured his Papa, when he fell from the ladder. Their love is imperishable, she vows, aged eighteen. She didn't cry, not much. 'I was so sorry, Odile, when I heard about what happened', says Michel, months later. 'I offer you my sympathy and condolences.' His voice had changed, Odile says, after all those years in hospital, after 37 operations, after convalescence, after so much rehab. He now walks on artificial legs and drives a car specially rigged up for invalids. 'His two feet in their polished shoes just rest on the floor. Like flatirons.' One afternoon he gives Odile and baby Christian a ride home, and insists on getting out of the car, moving his legs with his arms, extracting himself like a man climbing out of a trench he's dug. Another day, they go to a brasserie together; Odile has done up her hair, the first time since Stepan's death. They talk together, Odile and Michel; he says she has beautiful hair. 'All his words had to be hurled across the ravine of what had befallen him.' Do you remember the trip we made to Italy? he asks. She nods. She is 29, he 37.

In Michel's Renault 4 they take a trip to Paris because his prosthesis needs adjusting. In the Jura, a Peugeot 304, speeding round a bend, crashes into the back of Michel's Renault. Crippled cunt! the driver exclaims. Their car needs repairing so they spend a night in a strange B&B beside a river whose bed is almost dry. They never make it to Paris. 'I can die happily without ever seeing the capital', Odile says. 'We stayed for three nights at the mad hotel with the white geese.' And from their union came Marie-Noelle, and the limbs he'd lost were somehow returned to him in this small child's body.

'It is getting late and the light is already turning', says Odile near the story's end. 'The snow on the Gruvaz, facing west, is turning pink, the colour of the best rhubarb when cooked. I imagined we would come down to earth before it's dark, but Christian must know what he's doing. He's a national instructor, he came second in the European Championship of Hang-gliding and when I said to him, they've both gone to Annecy, they needn't know anything, need they? they won't be frightened, take me up this afternoon, the time's come, he simply replied: Are you ready?' 'Tell them, Christian, tell them when we land on the earth that there's nothing more to know.'

Maybe, maybe without knowing it, Berger's telling of Odile's story takes us one step nearer to *Lilac and Flag*, to the 'old wives' tale' of the urban underworld, to a world tellingly above ground and which might await Odile's own kids, Christian and Marie-Noelle. Indeed Odile herself could easily be the old wife in question and the two lovers, Lilac and Flag, the pet names of Zsuzsa and Sucus, her respective daughter- and son-in-law. Lilac and Flag are trying to tread their slippery way through the spectral city of Troy, a paradigmatic (post)modern city of expressways and concrete blocks, of money values and deceit, of immense freedom and brutal imprisonment.

Sucus lives with his mother and father on the fourteenth floor of an anonymous high-rise on the city's periphery; Papa Clement came from the village as a teenager and all his adult life worked opening oysters. One day Clement has a freak accident with a television set, gets badly burned and slips away in hospital. He had always wondered whether his son could find a job. 'There are no jobs', Sucus tells Papa on his deathbed, 'except the ones we invent. No jobs. No jobs.' 'Go back to the village, that's what I'd like to do', says Clement. 'See the mountains for the last-time.' Half the men in the ward, he says, were remembering either their village or their mothers'. Sucus' generation doesn't know the village, so could never go back; and yet, it cannot quite find itself in the alien city either. Sucus' generation can go neither backwards nor forwards: it has nostalgia for neither the past nor the future. And they're not prepared to take the same shit as their parents. Their expectations are different. But their prospects are non-existent.

Sucus once sold coffee outside the local prison, but somebody, in an organized heist, stole his flask; then he gets a job as a labourer on a building site. Yet he punches the hard-ass foreman and is sacked. In fact, all Sucus has in life are two things: his wits and his woman, Zsuzsa. Zsuzsa, though, has even less going for her and lives way out in a makeshift blue shack at Rat Hill, one of Troy's many shanties. Her brother, Naisi, has a sub-machine gun and is hip in his smooth leather boots yet gets in deep with neighbourhood toughs who sell drugs, and is later gunned down by the cops. ('We're born outside the law', Naisi says, 'and whatever we do, we break it.') Zsuzsa is a happy-go-lucky drifter, a sexy flirt who lives day to day and hand to mouth. She can't read words but knows how to read the signs in the street, and on people's faces. She calls her lover Sucus 'Flag' and wants him to call her 'Lilac', after the song: 'On the corner of the street/ The lilac's in flower/ So I have to pray and implore/ Lilac, oh Lilac/ Oh let me pass by/ Lilac, my sweet . . .'.

Together Lilac and Flag pilfer passports from an overnight train, from a first-class sleeper at so-called Budapest Station. Against all odds they consummate their union and spend the booty on a passionate night in an old-moneyed hotel that saw better days a century ago. (The ancient woman concierge even remembers the peasant Boris perishing with his sheep.) But, somehow, in among all the drama, we sense that menace lies ahead for at least one of them, that the great white death-ship is moored nearby at Troy's dockside, awaiting new passengers; and in this heavenly floating palace lifeboats aren't necessary because now everyone is out of danger.

From life experience, Lilac and Flag know that our cities are run by corrupt politicians and bent police, by shyster real estate corporations and financial institutions whose corruption is both blatant and legalized. They know the rules of the urban game are rigged against them. Their tragedy is a tragedy of arriving too late (or perhaps that's too early?). When their parents came there were still steady jobs, steady factory jobs, to be had. But those industries have gone bust or cleared out to someplace cheaper, to somewhere even more exploitable and expendable. Berger knows better than anyone how millions of peasants and smallholders across the globe are each year thrown off their rural land by big agribusiness, by corporate export farming; these people lose the means to feed themselves as well as the means to make a little money; so, as seventh men, they migrate to the city in search of work that's increasingly disappearing, migrating to an alien habitat they can little afford or understand.

Their sons and daughters understand this habitat better, well enough to know that now there are no decent jobs left, only insecure, underpaid work, and overworked workers everywhere in its Lazarus informal layers: busboys and valet parkers, waiters and barmen, cleaners and security guards, builders and buskers, hawkers and hustlers. A push–pull effect has taken hold, a vicious dialectic of dispossession, sucking people into the city while spitting others out of the centre, forcing poor urban old-timers and vulnerable newcomers to embrace each other out on the periphery, out on assorted zones of social marginalization, out on the global *banlieue*. This is the bigger old wives' tale that *Lilac and Flag* tells.

Perhaps it is not too surprising that the old woman who remains in the village, and who tells her story, does not like the city. For her, when push comes to shove, there are really only two types of people: there are peasants and there are those who feed off peasants. The old wife is wary of the city, of all the city stands for, of how its value system corrupts, of how its experience disrupts. On one level, an abstract level, Berger sees the promise of the city, sees the city as a place of mixing, as a site of dissidence, of seren-dipitous encounter, of compassionate solidarity; so his urban vision doesn't exactly tally with that of the old woman's. Yet on another level, a concrete level, Berger's city, too, is a city of Sodom and Gomorrah, the great whore Babylon. Here money and the city go hand in hand and each, in turn, seduce and destroy. (Part of the 'failure' of Picasso, remember, was also his metropolitan 'success': the Midas touch he had in the art world – in the urban art *business* – was, for Berger, the kiss of death to his creativity.) All who yearn for urban gold, and all who touch it, be they peasant or artist, ultimately perish.

Who is to say Berger is wrong to hold this vision of urban life today? Who is to say the intimacy of the city isn't a 'terrible intimacy' (as he put it in his essay 'Manhattan')? Who is to say that the tragedy of the city isn't a tragedy stemming from its people having hoped excessively, and having those hopes serially dashed? Berger plainly believes that urban people role-play more than rural people; they wear masks, have to wear masks, and the expression of the mask is usually sad and lost. Who is to say the same doesn't go for migration, for forced emigration to the city, for uprooting oneself from one's village homeland, for retaining an 'imaginary homeland', for dreaming of the return while knowing there can never be any return? Hopes are born on the site of loss, Berger says. But to emigrate, to have it foisted upon you, is, he thinks, 'always to dismantle the centre of the world, and so to move into a lost, disorientated one of fragments'.[3] The capitalist city feeds off this fragmentation, depends upon migrant labour to do its shittiest jobs, to have slave recruits for the rich. For the sake of good capitalist rationality, the city needs a dispensable (post)industrial reserve army in which those who were once the possessors of animals now become the animals themselves.

Whether one accepts or not this old wives' vision of the city, *Lilac and Flag* remains an oddly unfulfilling, frustrating denouement to Berger's peasant masterwork. One can never quite empathize with Zsuzsa and Sucus, with either Lilac or Flag; one can never quite believe in them as characters. They don't touch us the same way that the Cocadrille or Odile, or Marcel and Boris, touch us. Each of the former somehow enter us, move us, stir something in us, haunt us. Lilac and Flag do not do any of that. It is hard to know exactly why this is, why *Lilac and Flag* is not working as majestically as *Pig Earth* and *Once in Europa*. Perhaps it's because the subject-matter – the urban world – is a world Berger knows less about, knows with less proximity, with less intimacy.

In *Pig Earth* and *Once in Europa* we could smell the raw earth, feel the mountain dewdrop; in *Lilac and Flag* there is nothing to smell, and little to feel other than pain. Perhaps that's Berger's point: the desensitized nature of urbanity, the way it forces everybody to struggle against one another. But the danger with his Troy as a composite of all cities – of Athens and Geneva, of giant Latin American cities, of Paris and New York – Troy as a composite of every urban ill, is that we lose definition: Troy does not become so much a living place as a thinking concept, a tendentious declaration. And a Berger making self-conscious declarations, making blatant tendentious declarations, is a Berger peddling ideas rather than sharing experience.

Therein, perhaps, lies the real reason why we cannot quite get into Lilac and Flag why we cannot enter their world: in *Lilac and Flag*, Berger still seems to be harbouring *novelistic* ambitions, and these ambitions are difficult to shrug off. For here and there one loses the storytelling voice of the old wife and a more remote, more abstract voice – a *novelist's* voice – starts to be overheard: you're no longer engaged to listen but hectored into reading. At these moments, the book moves away from the spoken word and becomes self-aware of itself as a *written text*. The storyteller becomes as lost in the text as the peasant is lost in the city. The storyteller becomes like the migrant labourer who, between working and sleeping, wanders aimlessly through familiar backstreets and waste lots, helplessly searching for stories to tell. He's disturbed and distressed, unnerved by an unfamiliar lack of nature, and by an almost utter absence of animals.

5

Animal Humanism

'Did you ever see a hare in the morning, run a few seconds over the silvery frost, then stop in the silence, sit down on its hind legs, prick up its ears and look at the horizon? Its gaze seems to confer peace upon the entire universe . . . At this moment, it is a sacred animal, one that should be worshipped.'

Gabriele d'Annunzio in Gaston Bachelard, *The Poetics of Space*

'Animals are more interesting than us. Or, if you prefer, we're the less interesting animals. With us it's chaos. Not them. And with people there's no mystery.'

Marcel in *Jonas qui aura 25 ans en l'an 2000*

The peasant wandering around Troy's ghostly streets is the migrant labourer wandering through the pages of *A Seventh Man* (1975). The evenings are hardest, the lonely evenings. By day he works in a giant killing factory, an industrial abattoir, where the scale and speed of death astounds him: 80 cattle get slaughtered an hour, 150,000 a year. At home in his village he killed maybe a couple of animals a week, always by hand, deftly with a knife, eviscerating them, skinning them, looking them in the eye, feeling the warmth the carcasses give off, especially in winter. He would talk with a colleague or work silently, with pride, with little need to rush. He did everything himself; or they did everything themselves, if ever he worked with another. Whatever the animal – sheep, ox, cow or goat – he always thought about the meat being bought and the meat that would be eaten.

Perhaps he should be grateful he has a paying job, a city job. Though now it's unskilled, reduced to washing the heads of cows – only heads, after they have been scalped – hundreds of heads each day he'll wash, doing it till he's goggle-eyed. After work he returns to the lodging house, shared with fifteen other migrant labourers. When his relatives are fast asleep at home, he's traipsing lonely streets, lost in a lost urban world, one eerily bereft of animals, bereft of sheep and goats, horses and donkeys, hens and hares, those who sprint across the hoar frost. Sometimes he passes a dog on a lead, or a cat on a wall.

Where are all the animals? he wonders. Where does the invisible herd graze each night? Inside, he *feels* the disconnect outside. There is always a moment on his way to the city, a moment he never realizes at the time, when he passes on the bus a species of animal or bird he won't see again for many months: the last stork, the last donkey, the last pig. On the return journey, he will recognize the first of this species as a kind of sentinel. Meanwhile, the mechanical mass death of cows, slaughtered on a conveyor belt in perpetual motion, on hydraulic hide-pullers, on automatic hoists, is a mass death of the worker, his mass death, a death of the subject, a complicit estrangement: a living workplace in which animal and human alike get dismembered.[1]

In between *A Seventh Man* and *Pig Earth*, exactly in between, Berger published 'Why Look at Animals?' (1977). The essay partly tried to conjoin these two books, to bridge them, to understand the continuity between them and their discontinuity. Although it reads very assertively, very confidently, the groundbreaking 'Why Look at Animals?' is really voicing a series of hypotheses; it is a tentative intervention on Berger's behalf; it pinpoints the research lying ahead rather than that already accomplished; it poses open questions rather than offering solid solutions. At times the phrasing sounds awkward; at others ideas seem scattergun, deliberately thrown out to provoke. But it is the raw, occasionally clumsy style of 'Why Look at Animals?' that makes it still worthy of reading 30-odd years on.[2]

From the mid-1970s onwards animals would figure heavily in Berger's oeuvre, just as they would figure heavily in his everyday rural life. The two facets would march *ensemble*. Animals figure in his stories and critical articles, in his drawings and poetry, to the degree that Bergerland became a veritable Noah's Ark. Yet animals were always portrayed in conjunction with the human world, always done in the sense of what light the two parties can shed on one another, always done non-sentimentally, unflinchingly, in both directions. Berger's sympathy for animals is a peasant sympathy: he might be fond of his pig, raises it lovingly, caringly, and is glad to salt away its pork. 'What is significant, and is so difficult for the urban stranger to understand', says Berger, 'is that the two statements in that sentence are connected by an *and* and not by a *but*.'

'Nearly all modern techniques of social conditioning', Berger says in 'Why Look at Animals?', 'were first established with animal experiments.' The mechanical view of animals, the reduction of animals to work machines, to beasts of burden, thus predates its human application. Yet animal mechanization is part and parcel of the same process 'by which people have been reduced to isolated productive and consuming units'. In the 1880s F. W. Taylor, the infamous brainchild of 'scientific management' and 'time-in-motion' studies, made the reciprocity definitive, proposing that work be 'so stupid', 'so phlegmatic', that each worker 'more nearly resembles in his mental make-up the ox than any other type'.

Two centuries ago, perhaps longer, 'anthropomorphism' (attrib-uting human qualities to animals) was integral to the relationship between humans and animals, 'and was an expression of their proximity', says Berger. 'Anthropomorphism was the residue of the continuous use of animal metaphor. In the last two centuries', he thinks, 'animals have gradually disappeared. Today we live without them. And in this new solitude, anthropomorphism makes us doubly uneasy.' It's an uneasiness felt deep down in our migrant labourer, deep down in his being, felt as a *lack* of animals and a *lack* of content to his work with animals.

Much of 'Why Look at Animals?' actually reads like an animal equivalent of Marx's denunciation of worker alienation in the *Economic and Philosophic Manuscripts*. There, says Marx, human alienation comes about through *objectification*, through some sort of loss: a loss of object, a loss of activity, a disconnection between our sensuous inner life and our sensuous outer life, between what we do and how we feel about doing it, how we feel when we work. The disconnection is real enough, *objective*, created by a certain physical activity; yet it is equally one with existential implications: it is something *subjective*, a feeling of self-worth, of self-respect, or lack of it. 'The objectification of the worker in his product', Marx says, 'means not only that his labour becomes an object, an *external* existence, but that it exists *outside him*, independently of him and alien to him, and begins to confront him as an autonomous power; that the life which he has bestowed on the object confronts him as hostile and alien.'

In Berger's eyes the alienation between humans and other humans within the act of work is deeply bound up with the alienation of humans from animals. Each severing – human from other humans, humans from animals – symbolizes the loss of meaningful connection to nature, a *double estrangement* in which both parties lose something of themselves. Marx himself pinpoints the complex relationship existing between humans and animals, that we both, he says, live from 'inorganic nature', that our and their 'species-beings' resemble each other. Always an admirer of Darwin's evolutionary theory, it is little wonder that Marx, too, recognized how animals *interceded* between humans and our origins:

we are both like and unlike one another. (Molecular biologists, for example, have shown that we share with chimpanzees 99 per cent of their DNA. A dog, on the other hand, differs from a raccoon by 12 per cent.)

Animals look at humans in much the same way as they look at other animals: which is to say, attentively and warily. 'But by no other species except man will the animal's look be recognized as familiar. Other animals are held by the look. Man becomes aware of himself returning the look.' But what was once an expression of proximity, of integral relationship, of mutual connection, which helped humans cross the nature–culture divide – or at least find delicate dialectical mediation – is now broken, now seemingly severed for good.

In the seventeenth century René Descartes started the ball rolling with his mind–body dualism, his Cartesian partitioning, internalizing a separation *within* humans and hence that implicit in our relationship with animals. In dividing body and soul absolutely, Descartes 'bequeathed the body to the laws of physics and mechanics, and, since animals were soulless, the animal was reduced to the model of the machine'. Steadily and assuredly, industrial society and corporate capitalism completed the rupture. The internal combustion engine displaced draught animals in streets, fields and factories; urbanization and suburbanization transformed surrounding countryside, where field animals once roamed; wildness everywhere was domesticated. Eventually, says Berger, Descartes' model was stunningly surpassed.

Soon animals would not be so much meat as raw material for processed food and *things* wrapped in cellophane, *things* chopped up into morsels, *things* put into Styrofoam boxes, unrecognizable to people (particularly to children) as anything that was once living, once whole, once part of nature. Zoos began springing up in response to the withdrawal of animals from daily life. But the spectacle of animals in zoos, or at circuses, can only disappoint, says Berger: dull and lethargic behind bars, in cages, on leads, or hyperactive when performing artificially, we – dully and letharg - ically, sometimes hyperactively – look back, likewise imprisoned. The unnatural behaviour of animals in zoos and in circuses bears witness to our own alienated behaviour.[3]

Family visits to zoos rarely correspond to sighting the 'original' animal that a child has in miniature at home. Where is he? the child wonders of the caged animal. Why doesn't he move? Is he dead? Everywhere the real becomes *ir*real: painted prairies, painted rock ponds, painted jungle, plastic rocks, neon lights, muzak to soothe or to create drama where there isn't any, all done to create the illusion of reality, the real fake. What was once directly lived has now moved away into a representation. 'Everywhere animals disappear', Berger says. 'In zoos they constitute the living monu- ment of their own disappearance.' The behaviour of animals in captivity says bundles about us and about 'the stresses involved in living in consumer society'. Indeed, Berger reckons, 'all sites of enforced marginalization – ghettos, shantytowns, prisons, madhouses, concentration camps – have something in common with zoos'. Today the marginalization of animals also parallels ' the marginalization and disposal of the only class who, through - out history, has remained familiar with animals and maintained the wisdom which accompanies that familiarity: middle and small peasant'.

In 1980 'Why Look at Animals?' made it to the small screen in a curious way, inspiring an hour-long BBC *Omnibus* documentary, 'Parting Shots from Animals'. Again Berger teamed up with director Mike Dibb (in collaboration with Chris Rawlence) and they col - lectively drew sustenance from Grandville's *Public and Private Life of Animals*, a series of engravings and satirical texts that the great French caricaturist completed between 1840 and 1842. 'Weary of insult, ignominy, and the constant oppression of man', so Grandville's work began, 'we, the so-called Lower Animals, have at last resolved to cast off the yoke of our oppressors, who, since the day of their creation, have rendered liberty and equality nothing more than empty names.' Grandville's tone throughout is lampooning and slapstick, just like Berger's and Dibb's; and Grandville's illustrations of animals all dressed up in human garb – in smart bourgeois garb – stunningly lifelike yet unnervingly surreal and macabre, hammer home the sense of shock and outrage.

'The doom of the human race is sealed', the convening animals agree,

> its world-wide sway ended! The savage despots have driven us from our homes, hewn down our forests, burned our jungles, ploughed up our prairies, scooped out the solid world to build their begrimed cities, lay their railroads, warm their thin blood, roast our flesh for food. Torturing, slaying, and playing the devil right and left, men have trod the skins of my ancestors under foot, worn our claws and teeth as talismans, poisoned us, imprisoned us, dried and stuffed us, and set us to mimic our bold natures beside mummies in museums. Down with them, I say! Down with the tyrants!

The key Grandville engraving is from 1842: 'Animals Entering the Steam Ark'. The animals have had it up to here with us humans! Enough! They are off, back into the Ark, sorry to have ever made it aboard with us in the first place. Grandville illustrates the Great Departure, the parting scene of animals, who await a Mississippi-style steamboat at the quayside: a long line of different species, all sporting elegant human dress, file slowly onto the ramp. The image looks a lot like the mass immigrant arrival at Ellis Island. Only now the flow is animal and in the opposite direction, back to pre-civilization, fleeing the modern world of humans. We're off! The bear. The lion. The donkey. The camel. The cock. The pig. The fox. Exeunt . . .

'Parting Shots from Animals' is a documentary that would never get made today. It is too satirical, too sombre in mood, too ironical in tone, too ambiguous in meaning for a contemporary television that flourishes through smiley faces, easy answers and readymade solutions. The commentary is not upbeat, nor is there any happy ending. At times Berger's opening narrative is menacing, warning of an apocalypse *now*. But the apocalypse, once announced, suddenly goes silent, and what follows often has no narration at all, just an eerie vision with the sound turned down, an animal Armageddon: a white horse stands alone in a desolate field on a very dreary English day, surrounded by bones and giant fossils of his long-extinct brethren. He is the last of the animals, the only one who stayed – or the unfortunate one who missed the boat.

This is a film made by animals, on behalf of animals. Its producers, Grandville-like in the TV studio, wear animal masks and remind listeners that this is not so much a film about us – about what remains of animals – as about *you* – about what remains of us humans once the animals have all gone. We're not pleading for ourselves, the animals say; rather, we're pleading for *you*, for *you* (*us*) the watchers. Our obsolescence doesn't seem to matter to you. Your slaughterhouses are hidden, why should you be ashamed? You desire our wildness, our freedom, you're fascinated by us, yet you've imprisoned yourselves, tamed yourselves.

Although Dibb's documentary was inspired by 'Why Look at Animals?' Berger himself only came into the project later on, when looking at an initial rough cut. It was then, Dibb told me, that Berger had the brilliant idea, an insight which gave the film a sharper edge: he reversed the perspective and suddenly things came alive: using Grandville, 'Parting Shots from Animals' would be a film made by animals about humans, and not the other way around, hence the decision to wear animal masks in the cutting studio.

'Parting Shots from Animals' leaves gaping actual human attitudes towards animals. It does not judge; it only reveals. We love animals and we mistreat them, hunt them into extinction. We worship animals and we desire their fur, their tusks. We plainly have difficulty reconciling the 'and' here. In zoos, on safari and in taxidermy, we yearn to see animals as they really *are*. In 'Parting Shots', we actually visit a taxidermy factory where a dedicated stuffer restores dead animals to better-than-lifelike shape. Then we watch how stuffed beavers live in their 'natural' habitats, in plastic earth, buried amid plastic undergrowth; spotlights overhead help people know where to look. We even visit an enterprise specializing in 'real' reproductions of tiger skin, painstakingly produced through computer-aided design, permitting the dyes and patterning to be nigh on perfect. Almost in the same frame, we watch an endangered tiger bound majestically across our screens, its untamed savagery and power there for all to relish, there to inspire every intrepid car driver to fill up on Esso. 'We'll leave you now, alone', says the final voiceover of 'Parting Shots from Animals', 'we wish you sweet animal dreams.'

The abattoir where that seventh man works, killing 80 cattle an hour, is worlds removed from the peasants that kill a cow at the beginning of *Pig Earth*. In this latter world there are no contra - dictory 'buts', only complementary 'ands'. The peasants who kill the cow also calf the cow: their hands slaughter *and* create life. And they know the place of each, the 'continuity' of death *and* life. Berger plainly believes that peasants have a much more honest relationship with animals, perhaps even a more *natural* one. And their disappearance in modern human culture is related to the marginalization of animals in modern human culture. For today our relationship with animals, just like our relationship with other humans, is *hypocritical*.

One village slaughterhouse he describes in *Pig Earth* is run by an old man, his wife, and their 28-year-old son. They are about to kill a peasant's cow whose teats are decomposing; she cannot be milked anymore. Death has a reason, a name rather than a number. 'Now is the best moment', the peasant says. 'If I'd kept her another two months until she calved, we couldn't have milked her. And after the birth she would've lost weight.' The son and mother drag the cow in, hood her, place spring bolts against her head, rendering her passive, and then the son cuts her throat. A large animal dies as quickly as a small one. Blood floods to the floor, forming an enormous velvet skirt below. Next the son cuts out the tongue, which he will hang beside the head and liver.

The son learned his craft from his father, learned his speed. Now, though, the father has slowed down, so the son works with his mother; between them there's a complicity, a mutual understanding. The son slits each hind leg with a single stroke of a tiny knife and inserts the hooks; the mother presses the button to start up the electric hoist. The son severs and twists off the four hooves and tosses them into a wheelbarrow; the mother removes the udder. Then the son axes the breastbone like a woodcutter axes a tree. From that moment on, a threshold is crossed: the cow, no longer an animal, is transformed into meat, just as a tree at some point is transformed into timber. At the finish the meat is weighed on the scales. The peasant and slaughterer agree to nine francs a kilo. When the peasant returns home later that day, the spot his cow used to occupy is vacant. He is sad *and* does not cry. He will put a young heifer there instead. By next summer she will remember her spot; each morning and night, when she returns from milking, she'll waddle back to the place in the cowshed that is now hers . . .

In *Pig Earth* there is an old peasant woman, Hélène, who also has a special relationship with the dead and the living, in both its animal and human manifestations. She goes to the cemetery to remember her dead husband and dead father. It is La Toussaint (All Saints' Day), 1 November, when across France people in villages remember the dead. They remember the dead in cities, too, of course, when loved ones likewise put chrysanthemums at gravesides.

But in rural life the proximity of the dead to the living is perhaps more deeply felt, perhaps more actively remembered. In rural life as well the dead perhaps more severely judge the living. Yet as flecks of snow fall like sawdust, creating life, especially new animal life, preoccupies Hélène. A great whiteness will soon cover us, she says. Soon it will be too late, too cold, and she will have fewer kids to sell in the springtime. There's still time, she tells one of her goats, after putting a pot of flowers on her father's grave. Let's go, she says, dragging her on a rope. You good-for-nothing carcass of a goat, let's go.

Darkness falls; it's freezing outside. Now the snow tumbles in large flakes. They step gingerly across a narrow path with a sheer drop on one side, a steep rock face of 350 metres. They stop on the *alpage* and Hélène starts to call – a shrill, sharp, short call, punctuated by silence. The cry rings out over the valley, disappears into the dark mountainous void. She cries again, and again. And then suddenly, in the silence, there is another call not far away. Hélène's goat responds herself, calling out to the invisible he-goat. He cries again, a cry that sounds like a bagpipe, a lament of breath emitted from a bag of skin. (The Greeks called the cry of the he-goat *tragoida*, from which the word *tragedy* derives.) Before long the he-goat appears, with an unhurried gait, his four great horns entwined with each other. He begins licking the female, smelling her. Soon his little red-tipped penis, looking like a ballpoint pen, pops out from its tuft of hair.

Jesus, Marie and Joseph, Hélène murmurs. Hurry! Get on with it! Her hands are frozen. The he-goat taps the flank of the she-goat with one of his forelegs, then he taps her other flank with his other foreleg and, when she is ready, when in position, he mounts and enters her. Nothing else under the starless night moves, save the snowflakes and his haunches. He thrusts in and out. His entire body shakes momentarily. Hélène presses with all her might on the goat's back, to ensure the sperm is retained. After a while his forelegs slide off and the two females set off back to the village. Lazy good-for-nothing carcass of a goat, Hélène repeats. Don't lose it! The wind blows the snow in whorls, writes Berger, and Hélène, for fear of slipping, walks holding the goat's collar.

Berger's animal fascination has another, more private side to it, a *personal* and intellectual interest in animals: he is an ardent drawer of animals – not only in words, as we have seen here, but in pencil and crayon, in charcoal and artist's ink. He has even sketched a he-goat, in Galicia, Spain, a he-goat sitting under a donkey. The he-goat has horns like the one in Hélène's tale from *Pig Earth*. The goat is standing there, in rough outline, beside a donkey with a big head, heavily shaded in pencil, suggesting the lad's a chocolate brown. The donkey's ears are splayed, rotating on their axes, twirling around the way they do when donkeys shoo away flies. Head and ears move in strange donkey unison, in opposite directions, contrapuntally, much as a wave and particle work with and against one another in subatomic physics. Gentle pencil strokes and finger smudging of darker shadings capture the spirit of this flow and stasis.[4]

It's perhaps not too hard to imagine Berger climbing over a fence and sitting with his back against a tree trunk, maybe an apple tree, sitting in rural peace one summer's day with his sketchpad and pen. He is drawing a line and then smudging it with his wet index finger, focusing on the living object before him, dissecting it in his mind's eye, putting it back together again on the page; each line drawn is a stepping-stone from which he proceeds to the next. Sitting against a tree, looking at and drawing animals, musing on animals in a shady spot of a meadow, evinces Berger's almost Bachelardian appreciation of the animal kingdom, a Bachelard whose influence Berger has readily acknowledged.

Himself of peasant stock, *bourguignon* peasant stock, Gaston Bachelard is the great philosopher of reverie, the grey-bearded prophet-professor who runs to romantic poets and novelists for inspiration rather than to fellow academics. Bachelard, like Berger, loves to understand the reverie and poetics the natural elements inspire, reveries of earth and air, reveries of water and mountains, reveries of animals. A dreamer who lets their musings follow an animal's line of vision, Bachelard says in the wonderful *The Poetics of Space*, 'will experience the immensity of outstretched fields in a higher key'. In looking at animals, in looking into their eyes – eyes no longer on the look out, eyes no longer a rivet of an animal machine – we can, says Bachelard, witness 'waves of calm' and 'the dialectics of immensity and depth', 'an instant when animal peace becomes identified with world peace'.

In looking at Berger looking at animals, looking at them the way Bachelard did, we can also discover waves of Berger's calm, another facet of action man Berger himself, a lesser known facet perhaps: the man of repose, out in his garden, or in a field somewhere, or up a mountain, a mellow Berger, a fatherly and increasingly grand - fatherly figure alone with his thoughts, daydreaming in private with his pen and blank white page. This is a Berger sat against a tree who shares his company with a donkey and a he-goat, or with a few cows or a stray dog. With them, he himself has said, there's a substratum of what you would call *gratitude*. And yet that man of calm, that man of reverie, that man who peddles an animal humanism, can he still be Marxist?

One might wonder, meanwhile, how much of Berger there is in another drawer of animals: Marcel, the peasant smallholder from Alain Tanner's *Jonas qui aura 25 ans en l'an 2000* (1976). Scripted by Berger and Tanner, *Jonas* is the most successful Swiss film ever made, with over two million viewers worldwide. Eight quirky '68ers try to tread their honest way through failed hopes and economic slump; they want no part in either hollow consumerist promises or in 1970s fatalism. Tender and ironic, idealist and bittersweet, each character quietly resists, gently exerts their admirable insubordination:

Marie, the flaky checkout girl who undercharges her poor elderly customers; Marco, the bizarre teacher who gives history lessons with blood sausages; Max, the gambler and disillusioned ex-Maoist; Madeleine, the nymphomaniac experimenting with the Kama Sutra; Mathieu, the 'frictionally' unemployed, class-conscious shit-shoveller; Mathilde, his wife, inside whose belly lies Jonas; Marguerite, the earthy farmwife; and, of course, Marcel the sketcher of animals, Marguerite's husband, the man who prefers animals to humans because with us there is too much chaos, less interest, no mystery . . .

Marcel's smallholding is on the edge of Geneva and he sells his veg at the city's farmer's market. In Berger and Tanner's character notes, Marcel is said to be the film's craziest personality, living least in the 'real world'. By nature he is an ascetic, and a free spirit. He photographs animals and then makes naive sketches from each picture; his drawings are confined to his own private room; his photos, though, cover the kitchen wall, a kitchen in which much of the drama of *Jonas* unfolds. (Even though Marcel's passion is for the animal kingdom, there are some wonderfully natural and touching human exchanges occurring around his and Marguerite's farmhouse kitchen table, replete with its chequered tablecloth.)

In one scene a banker arrives at the farm wanting to purchase Marcel's land. The city is encroaching on the countryside, and Marcel is sitting on expensive land, land ripe for redevelopment, for 'higher', more 'exploitable' commercial activities: high-tech industry, offices, rich people's housing. The banks, as well as the real estate men, want Marcel out. (*Jonas* shows how migrant workers not only go to the city, but how the city also goes to migrant workers, or at least to the migrant worker's homeland.) 'Have you ever heard a nightingale?', Marcel asks the man from the bank, who is dressed in a neat suit and tie. 'Yes, a few times', he says. 'From your bed?' Marcel wonders. 'Unfortunately, no, I live in the city', the banker replies. 'But in twenty years, dear sir', the banker adds, 'your children will not be fattening on nightingales. Insofar as they can be eaten, of course . . .'.

'Oh yes, they can be eaten', says Marcel. 'In pâté, or spitted, that's even better.' 'In twenty years they'll be poisoned by your chemicals', Marguerite chips in. 'I'm not in chemicals myself', the banker says. 'Some of your brothers are', Marcel interrupts. 'And it's you who give them the money. And to the people exterminating the whales . . . you rip the ozone from the sky, you lengthen pigs so that they'll have two extra sets of ribs, you run highways across sugar-beet fields, calves stinking of penicillin, blind chickens . . .'.

In a later scene, a wishful-thinking, revenge scene filmed in black and white, Marcel and Marguerite and two Italian migrant workers (Geneva is full of them) burst into the banker's downtown office, invading his pen-pushing, money-making cleanliness. They sully it with something antithetical to that world, a symbol of their world, a 'squalid' world that city slickers want to cleanse, want to take back: a pig, a dirty little pig, squealing and snorting, a pig who knows the value of money. The banker shrieks in horror as the two Italians coarsely order him out the way, so they can put the pig in his rightful place, in the boss's leather chair . . .

Marcel is Berger's otherworldly alter ego, *son semblable, son frère*, another drawer of animals on the sly; Marcel the man who, in another life, might have been a mystic. Yet it is equally true that Berger's other double in *Jonas* is Max, the embittered but not quite defeated nor exhausted ex-militant. Indeed, we might say that the two personalities – Marcel and Max – coexist in Berger as an *and* and not as a *but*. The quiet sketcher of animals and the engaged organic intellectual are thus two facets of the donkey's ears, the particle and wave of Berger's own persona, his animal-humanism incarnate. It is Max, after all, who tips off Marcel about the bank's land deal; it is Max (played by Jean-Luc Bideau, who even resembles a 40-something Berger) whose vision of history is vaster than any

other character in the film, and who is still inspired by the
dampened hopes of 1968. In his character there is something at
once life-affirming and tragic: he's a man as much at home on the
barricade as around the farmhouse kitchen table.

That is perhaps why the quiet sketcher of animals has an
eye that isn't entirely passive or inactive. That is why when that
sketcher draws a simple, almost naive image of a dog with a silver
pen, with a sort of translucent pen, a dog whose tongue hangs out,
there's a vaster vision of history getting barked here. That vaster
vision becomes even more vivid set against a black background,
on black paper. Berger, of course, has sketched such a little dog,
a mischievous little dog who pants and dances off the black page.
What is this dog's name? KING. He's a stray who hangs around
town dumps: he's an urban dog, cocky, seen a lot, many vagrants,
many homeless people – SDF (*sans domicile fixe*) – some near the
Elf garage near the expressway M.1000.

King is Berger's aberrant magical realist portrayal of homelessness from 1999, not a novel as such but a 'street story', framed from
the standpoint of a sly talking dog; or a dog who muses aloud,
a dog, like all dogs, says Berger, who dreams of forests, of forest
blackness, of running along forest trails. 'When the sun set, the
forest was filled with blackness', says King, 'not with the colour
black, but the mystery, the invitation of black. Blackness as in
a black coat, as in black hair, as in a touching you didn't know
existed.' 'King', bawls Vica, a homeless woman, 'keep your mouth
shut, you don't know what you're talking about.' 'I'm talking about
the colour black', King, the dog, replies, 'and about sex.'[5]

Like Berger's eponymous dog star, *King: A Street Story* is a sly,
brilliantly conceived, linguistically dazzling vision of reality from
the bottom up; framed not so much from street level as from dog
level, at the visual and conceptual canine plane, at the interstices
between two different sets of the visible that Berger attributes to
the dog order. 'Dogs, with their running legs, sharp noses and

developed memory for sounds', he says, 'are natural frontier experts of these interstices.'[6] Dogs somehow sense this strange territory between frames of life, between the split-second flickering that lies beyond human perception. In *King* Berger tries to momentarily freeze this perception, to transmit an animal understanding of human suffering, an understanding more akin to that of a child's. The look of dogs, of dogs' eyes, is urgent and mute, Berger says, finely attuned to seeing the visible order (or disorder) of human misery and another invisible order in which hope resides. King is always urging the homeless couple Vico and Vica to go back to where they came from, or else to go forward, to enter into this other order of things, an order in which he, King, can be their guide-dog, their dog-Christ.

After visiting homeless shantytowns in Alicante, Spain, Berger insisted that the narrator of *King* had to be a dog. The number of stray dogs wandering around, seemingly gravitating towards human deprivation, seemingly comforting the most humanly deprived, struck him as somehow significant – politically and poetically. Dogs and human beings seemed to be barking together, barking their heads off into the wind. In Alicante, as in King's shanty of Saint Valéry, everyone needs a madness to find their balance after the wreck. 'It's like walking with a stick', King says. 'Madness is a third leg. Me, for instance, I believe I'm a dog. Here nobody knows the truth.' At Saint Valéry, the barking voice travels right up to the constellations, and its star-sign is all too human. 'A bark is a voice which breaks out of a bottle', writes Berger,

> saying, I'm here. The bottle is silence. The silence broken, the bark announces, I'm here.
>
> After a while you forget you're barking, and when this happens you hear the others, you hear the chorus of barks and, although not one of them has changed and each is distinct, so distinct that it can break a heart, the barking is saying something different

now, it's saying, We're here! and this *We're here* blows on an almost dead memory, and it revives like the dead ashes of a fire glowing again thanks to a night wind, and the memory is of the pack, of fear, of the forest, and of food.[7]

Maybe Berger can hear this barking sat against the apple tree, a barking heard as the sketcher sketches in the sunshine. The silence he hears is thus never a dead silence, never a silence without fear, never a silence without a desire to live, to make noise, to draw what is invisible, to question and to speak out. Even in the calm, even as the donkeys approach him, as they size him up with their questioning glances, even in the summer meadowland, Berger never forgets the winter wasteland. 'They wander away, heads down, grazing, their eyes missing nothing; I watch them, eyes skinned . . .'. Yes, he says, Yes, I am still Yes amongst other things a Marxist . . .[8]

6

Amongst Other Things a Marxist

'My political views are an intrinsic part of my view of the truth and of
how I see life, and if I ever wrote anything, if I ever wrote two lines in
which they were not implicit, I would be ashamed of myself.'
John Berger in the film *A Fortunate Man*

'He who fights can lose; he who doesn't fight has already lost.'
Bertolt Brecht cited by Berger in 'Les vivants et les morts' (France TV 2)

Berger's is a finely textured humanist, animal and mineral
Marxism, infused with a Blakeian impulse for mystical trans-
cendence yet full of Proudhonist love of the artisan, mindful
of an archaic mode of production that lives on inside advanced
capitalism – one that continues to fight back, that now serves to
subvert from below the globalism imposed from above. Marx says
rural life is 'idiotic' and the peasantry a 'sack of potatoes'; Berger
sees the world's peasantry and indigenous struggles as vital
ingredients for new organic nourishment, for anti-corporate
self-determination, for new eco-sovereignty in an era of delocali -
zations, agrotoxins and transgenic seeds. At the same time Marx,
who prophesied and analysed free-market devastation, mass
accumulation by dispossession, has not lost any of his brilliant
insight for giving progressives political bearings, for offering
indispensable radical coordinates. How is it possible, Berger asks,
not to heed Marx?

Berger's Marxism has always been a dissident Marxism. In the 1960s he was close to the Prague Spring and incredulous of Politburo communism even before the Soviet invasion of Hungary in 1956. (In the early 1950s Berger had read, seen and supported works by renegade Soviet artists, people like Ernst Neizvestny, Marxist artists defiant of Party-line authoritarianism.) In recent years Bergerian Marxism, characterized by its support of Sub-comandante Marcos and the Palestinians, is unrepentant in its autonomous desire for a politics of authenticity, which sometimes steers Berger over towards Spinoza, Marx's preferred philosopher, the philosopher of the constitutive power of the subject. 'The problem with Marxism', Berger once admitted to *The Sunday Times* (31 August 2008),

> is there is no real space for ethics . . . there is plenty of space in it for the struggle of justice against injustice, but the notion that an act is good or bad in itself – there is no space for that. There is no space for that which is outside time or, if you wish, for the eternal. There is the possibility [however] of it being combined with another philosophical view which is not simply materialist.

Antonio Gramsci, Lukács, Benjamin and the Frankfurt School are all palpable in Berger's Marxist aesthetic theory, and the great bearded sage's concept of 'commodity fetishism' lies at the nub of *Ways of Seeing*, of its tearing down of the 'aura' of the artistic masterpiece; getting back to the realm of production, even to the realm of the production of the migrant worker (as in *A Seventh Man*), exhibits Berger's marked penchant for *marxiant* analyses – as a means of comprehending the world and of changing that world. Like the best Marxists, Berger's Marxism is not contrived or banal, abstruse or simplistic. Almost always it remains unstated and implicit, whether in his essays or fiction; almost always it is the guiding (and joining) thread rather than the actual fabric of his writings; almost always it is an intrinsic part of his radical politics.

In a way there are two prongs to Berger's Marxism: an 'objective', colder, analytical side, investigating structural or broad historical dynamics; and a warmer humanist side when looking at the role of agency and subjectivity *within* those overall dynamics. Needless to say Berger's polemical sway is most effective when it somehow melds these two realms together in an engaging organic whole. Therein the search for 'deep' objectivity is a curious process: only after close identification with an issue or person, only after a great deal of *subjective* feeling for it or them, can any writer or analyst, Berger thinks, attain a more informed and total objectivity. Only after one has stripped away different levels of *reification* can one really begin to approach a subject in its true authenticity.

Lukács' influence on Berger is again palpable, Lukács who developed the concept of reification as a powerful amalgam of Marx's youthful theses on alienation and his mature theory of fetishism. In *History and Class Consciousness* (1923), Lukács says his intention 'is to base ourselves on Marx's economic analyses and to proceed from there to a discussion of the problems growing out of the fetish character of commodities, both as an objective form and also a subjective stance corresponding to it'. Under capitalism relations between people (as both workers and consumers) tend to take on a 'phantom objectivity', assume a state of relations between 'things'. The world of 'living' social relations gets thingified into the 'dead' world of money and commodities; hence the riddle of the commodity, with its 'automatic fetish' (Marx), is, according to Lukács, 'the central structural problem of capitalist society in all its aspects'.

Reification permeates all social life, Lukács says: it permeates politics and culture and is perpetuated by media and ideology, by subtle subconscious messages as well as conscious brute force. Ruling classes prosper from reification since ordinary people, deceived by and submissive to reification, are unable to grasp fully their real conditions of life. 'Reification', Lukács thinks,

> is the necessary, immediate reality of every person living in capitalist society. It can be overcome only by constant and constantly renewed efforts to disrupt the reified structure of existence by concretely relating to the concretely manifested contradictions of the total development, by becoming conscious of the *immanent meanings* of these contradictions [emphasis added].

The 'immanent meanings' of the art world preoccupied Berger in *Ways of Seeing*. His other way of seeing art was thus an attempt to release art, to demystify art, to blast apart reification, to expose what the commodity form and money relations have done to art. A critical approach to art, a critical consciousness of art, could then challenge the reified realm of capitalist artistic production and reproduction. Once a critical conscious is developed, art and art theory can help people paint their own lives.

Where Berger parts comradely company with Lukács is, perhaps, in believing that capitalism is never seamless. Berger's mind is nourished by openness, not closure: even in the reified totality of contemporary capitalism there are always holes, inconspicuous little cracks; commodification is real enough, but it has not over - whelmed everything, can never overwhelm everything. There is always *porosity* in culture and art, in thinking and living, in every - day life. Wherever there is reification there are victims; but wherever there are victims there is also resistance; and wherever there is resistance, Berger knows, there is always hope.

Reification is a form of unfreedom. It can express itself subtly or blatantly; often it does both at the same time. Unfreedom lies at the core of *A Seventh Man*, Berger's most overtly Marxist text. 'This unfreedom', Berger says in a language reminiscent of Lukács', 'can only be fully recognized if an objective economic system is related to the subjective experience of those trapped within it.' To recognize unfreedom is perhaps to struggle to take away its power; to resist within that unfreedom is already to pursue its dialectical other, something freer. If *A Seventh Man* is a story of unfreedom, it is equally a story of exploitation, done with words and images (again Jean Mohr's), to be read and looked at on their own terms.

Like a lot of Berger's political tracts, *A Seventh Man*'s morality play comes from its avoidance of moralizing. What gets presented is an 'objective' vision of the European migrant worker, one that approaches the subject-matter intimately, in flesh and blood and tears, placing flexible and dispensable labour-power in its broader context of postwar capitalist development, of postwar capitalist crisis, of postwar capitalist 'laws of motion', doing it subjectively yet with a certain emotional distance, as Marx did in *Capital*.[1]

That 'thing', that labour-power, is likewise a He (and sometimes a She), a He and She who journey to Paris and Geneva, to Frankfurt and Stuttgart, to Berlin and Amsterdam, to Vienna and Stockholm, to Lyon and Lausanne, coming from Portugal and southern Italy, from Spain and Turkey, from the Balkans and Greece, from pig earth villages everywhere in Europe's periphery. Those Hes and Shes were once temporary expedients, there to solve temporary labour 'shortages' in lowly sectors of metropolitan economies (too degrading for native populations); now these stopgap migrants are permanent necessities, vital levers of economic expansion and private profitability, essential for vested capitalist business interests. Left behind are life-worlds *actively* underdeveloped by structural and institutional forces still at large. 'Modern rural poverty', Berger says in *A Seventh Man*,

has a social rather than a natural basis. The land becomes barren though lack of irrigation or seed or fertilizers or equipment. The unproductivity of the land then leads to unemployment or underemployment . . . The economic relations which intervene between land and the peasants – the share-cropping system, the system of land tenure, the money-lending system, the marketing system – come to be seen as part of the barrenness of the land.

So, with little choice, they come. They leave because there is nothing there anymore, nothing except their *everything*, which no longer feeds their families. It is not people who migrate but machine-minders, sweepers and diggers, cleaners and drillers, waiters and busboys, cement mixers and bricklayers, crane drivers and road-builders. Migration, says Berger, represents an 'unequal exchange' involving a transfer of valuable economic resources – human labour – from poor to rich countries; workers come ready-made, readily exploitable, because their costs of reproduction have been borne by their home countries. With each arriving migrant an underdeveloped economy subsidizes a developed one. And the most energetic, able-bodied and enterprising generation is lost at home, further depriving donor economies. The promise of skills, meanwhile, is a hollow promise: invariably migrants partake in the most unskilled of manual labour, learned on the job, usually in a day, gaining nothing, deskilled from everything they once knew before. All deep ontological connection with work is consequently foregone.

In *A Seventh Man* Berger manages to put together early and mature Marx in a graphically *human* narrative. (Mohr's docu - mentary photojournalism is once again indispensable in this regard.) On the one hand, the Marx of *Capital* shines through, the Marx who theorized the 'industrial reserve army of labour', or 'relative surplus population' as he sometimes labelled them, whose presence regulates the general movement of wages. Wages are not 'determined by the variations of the absolute numbers of the working population', Marx says, 'but by the varying propor - tions in which the working class is divided into an active and reserve army, by the increase or diminution in the relative amount of surplus population, by the extent to which it is alternately absorbed and set free'. The migrant labourer, tapped during growth cycles, sent home during downturns, comes into his (or her) own, forming the 'stagnant' and 'floating' surplus populations of Marx's industrial reserve army. The stagnant form, characterized 'by a maximum of working time and a minimum of wages', is 'constantly recruited from workers in large-scale industry and agriculture that have become redundant, and especially from decaying branches of industry where handicrafts is giving way to manufacture, and manufacture to machinery'. Meanwhile the floating population is sucked in and out of jobs, on-call and frequently paid by the day or by the task, a labour force both contingent and convenient (for enterprises); their sole regularity is the irregularity of work.

On the other hand, where Berger's originality as a Marxist lies is in concretely bedding down worker *alienation*. His story of the migrant worker is never left dangling at the abstract plane of economic analyses. In the text and images we *feel* the lostness and emptiness of the migrant labourer experience, their alienated subjectivity on the job. We can literally feel the existential melt-down, the philosophical homesickness of the man pushing his nocturnal trolley in the bowels of an anonymous office block, somewhere in the dimly lit basement of European capital; we can smell the ammonia-cleansed floors, the toxic humiliation. Though even here, even amid the reek of chemicals and the lonely, fluor - escent sadness, we can sense the stoicism of the pusher, the man behind the trolley, his *endurance* intact in spite of it all, his face shadowed but always (or nearly always) his will lit up. Surplus value has a face: it smiles and laughs, cries alone, sleeps somewhere, dreams and daydreams, makes coffee in barracks, withdraws into personal anticipations, into memories. The text and the pictures tell all, reveal all, reveal the labour-power that also plays the guitar and dances a polka.

Human agency is delicately positioned within Berger's heterodox Marxism: the defiance and endurance of human agency, its free will in the face of 'objective' constraints, its psychological mysteries, its contradictions, its needs. One has certain choices and one can choose to resist. One can fight and lose, battle as seventh men or as fortunate men; but for those who do not even try to fight, their battle is already lost. *A Seventh Man*'s Marxism is obvious, even if the role of agency within it is rather subdued, somewhat under-stated; *A Fortunate Man*'s agency is more obvious, even if the role of Marxism within it is rather subdued, somewhat understated. Yet both are clearly Marxist texts – in the sense of Berger's unconventional Marxism, a Marxism as unconventional as John Sassall's medical unconventionality, the fortunate doctor who commands the central place in Berger and Mohr's 1967 book, now almost a classic piece of Marxist ethnography.

A Fortunate Man is a political book without any reference to politics as such. It is a book that, as ever with Berger, defies easy classification. It is a non-fiction book with lots of imaginative flair. It is a creative artist's rendering of the truth, of a truth. In many ways, if there is any peer, it is a European equivalent of a genre that Americans were in the 1960s already calling 'New Journalism', pioneered by the likes of Truman Capote's *In Cold Blood*, Tom Wolfe's *Electric Kool-Aid Acid Test* and Norman Mailer's *The Armies of the Night*. As in New Journalism, Berger was applying to realist reportage certain techniques from fiction, from the novel, from storytelling: the same devices, the same plot constructions and rhetorical tropes. Screens get stripped away and the writer is one step closer to absolute involvement in the narrative, one step closer to absolute involvement with the reader. All traditional notions of 'objectivity' are somehow tossed out of the window.

In *A Fortunate Man* Berger is trying to express and give docu-mentary shape to the parameters of free will, to self-affirmation and self-expression, to one man's striving for *universality* – as Berger puts it. The book's central character, its real-life character, its larger than life character, the humanly vulnerable Dr John Sassall, is not a political being: he is a 'simple' country doctor who spends most days (and nights) trudging across muddy fields and along forest paths with his little black instrument bag in hand, serving an economically depressed forest community that is neither traditionally proletarian nor classically rural. Sassall is a one-man mobile clinic, performing appendix operations on kitchen tables, delivering babies in caravans, hauling out woodcutters from beneath felled trees. He is a man at home in the midst of crises – in illness and distress, in dying and decay, in accident and emergency.

Why was Sassall chosen? How did Berger and Jean Mohr, who were both living in Geneva at the time (1966–7), come to know said country doctor? Berger had known him before, when he had lived in Britain, and already knew how Sassall thrived off crises. The proximity to death drove Sassall on, made him feel *more alive*. For Berger, he was the right man to frame the central theme of *A Fortunate Man*: the dignity and detail of people struggling individually and collectively for continuity and survival. Neither Berger nor Mohr knew beforehand how their New Journalism might shape up, how the black and white photos might comple - ment the text. As always their collaboration would be negotiated. What they did know, however, was how those photos figuring in *A Fortunate Man* could not speak themselves, could not tell: they could only hint at what was going on in people's heads, what was on Sassall's mind. It was Berger's text, and Berger's text alone, that could offer judgement, give explanation, or else try to.

Sassall is constantly overworked and proud of it, wouldn't want it any other way. He has consciously *chosen* to live and work here, in this manner, and to a large extent has liberated himself in doing so, liberated himself from received convention and ascribed social etiquette.[2] He is his own man, empowered in what he does, in what he achieves, in how he fails. By society's miserable standards,

Berger says – by the standards of the miserable lives his patients lead – by feeling connected to how he works, pursuing what he wants to pursue, he is a *fortunate* man, the very opposite of an unfortunate man, a seventh man.[3]

Sassall spends a lot of time listening to the sick and needy, to the lonely and depressed, empathizing with them, reaching out to them, breaking down conventional distance between specialist and patient. He sits with anguished patients, at the bedside of the almost dead, the terminally ill both ready and not ready to die. He comforts close relatives; he passes quiet hours with schizophrenics who want to kill themselves, with hysterics he knows he will never reach. Sassall gets depressed sometimes, too. His approach to medicine, Berger says, is dialectical, often veering towards psycho - therapy. He never separates an illness from the 'total personality' of the patient; illness, for Sassall, is often a form of expression rather than a surrender to natural breakdown.

In spare moments Sassall reads Freud, and so far as he is able he psychoanalyses his own character traits. Once Sassall read Conrad and was drawn to his poetry and imagination, to casting off in the open sea of possibility, to tough, dramatic adventure. Now Sassall's ocean is medicine, another uncharted continent of adventure, both conscious and unconscious; there, his imagination can roam and express itself; there, he cures others to cure himself. His sense of self-mastery, Berger says, is 'fed by the ideal of striving towards the *universal*', to becoming a whole person. 'The enemy of the universal man', writes Berger, 'is the division of labour. By the mid-nineteenth century the division of labour in capitalist society had not only destroyed the possibility of a man having roles: it denied him even one role, and condemned him instead to being part of a mechanical process.'

Sassall is a fortunate exception to this rule. To that extent he is a privileged man. His privilege is not about an income or a car or a house. Sassall is privileged because of the way he can think and talk; he is privileged because he is 'indifferent to success'; he is privileged because he demands the right to think for himself, the right to be theoretical, the right to generalize and to understand life in all its weird complexity. His privilege is that he has an insatiable appetite for knowledge (and self-knowledge), continually extending and amending his awareness of what is possible. Inevitably, self-development and self-knowledge brings Sassall closer to death, to finality, which is all around him. 'Whenever I am reminded of death', Berger quotes Sassall saying, 'and it happens every day – I think of my own, and this makes me try to work harder.'

Fifteen years after the publication of Berger's *A Fortunate Man*, Dr John Sassall took his own life. The storyteller once again reads what is in black; the Death secretary files away his cold case. 'The day before yesterday', Berger wrote in 1982 in 'The Secretary of Death', 'a close friend of mine killed himself by blowing out his brains.' That friend was John Sassall.[4] And yet, as Berger qualifies in an updated postscript of *A Fortunate Man*, there was nothing *unfortunate* about this last act, nothing *negative* about it. Suicide does not necessarily imply a critique of life by putting an end to life; rather, it can, Berger says, reveal a certain destiny of that life. True, both Sassall's life and Berger's book can never be read in the same way as when Sassall was alive; Berger says as much in what now reads as an eerily prescient anti-conclusion to his narrative. What if Sassall were dead? Berger asks. 'A man's death makes everything certain about him. Of course, secrets may die with him . . . Death changes the facts qualitatively but not quantitatively.' What he wrote, Berger says of *A Fortunate Man*, still stands. Though if he ever reread the text, Berger's tenderness for Sassall's plight, for his life and work, would only increase.

Sassall was not condemned: he condemned himself. Perhaps that is the real story Berger told. A life lived on Sassall's own terms, set to his rules, completed according to those rules, consummated by his own fair hand. The final gesture he makes, the last poetic act in the heart of darkness, meant he chose his own death as well as his own life. The line between the two might be thinner than one imagines – though one suspects that Sassall knew this all too well himself. His proximity to death always made him aware of the precariousness of life, his own included, and in this regard Sassall shares a lot in common with Ernst Neizvestny, another fortunate man, an artist from Moscow, a Marxist who once told Khrushchev: 'you're talking to a man who is perfectly capable of killing himself at any moment'. From a Marxist standpoint there is perhaps more in common between these two men and Berger's two books on these men – *A Fortunate Man* and *Art and Revolution: Ernst Neizvestny, Endurance, and the Role of Art* (1969) – than immediately seems apparent.

Death, of course, animates both men and both books. Yet the will to live, the extraordinary adaptability and obstinacy to live and work, *endurance* to work, seem equally to have defined the fortunate doctor and go on defining the Russian artist. Death and mutilation, people with torn and missing limbs, wounded and moaning figures, the survivors and the maimed, the suicides, are everywhere in Neizvestny's life-affirming drawings, etchings and sculptures. The poles of Neizvestny's imagination, Berger says, are life and death – just as they were for Sassall:

> a polarity so fundamental and general that it can seem banal. Yet for Neizvestny it is particular and unique. It was first established by his own near-death when [during the Second World War] he lay for an immeasurable period of time on the ground where the small battle had been fought behind German lines.

Neizvestny was believed dead. Gravely injured by a bullet that entered his chest and exploded in his back, he nonetheless survived, amazingly survived. His will to live had been so immense, so desperate, that he had scrambled out of the valley of the shadow of death; he had come close enough to death that henceforth he could always measure the fine line distancing us from it.

From the late 1960s onwards, for years and years, Berger and Neizvestny corresponded. But because neither man could use his own language, they exchanged, as a private lingua franca, little sketches. In the early 1970s Neizvestny repeatedly applied for a travel visa; he wanted to accept overseas invitations to participate in debates about his art. Fifty times his application was turned down. Then, in March 1975, he asked for an emigration visa: he did not want to leave the USSR, yet to continue to work, to grow as an artist, he was forced to. Finally, in the spring of 1976, Neizvestny received his visa, departing first for Switzerland (Zurich) and afterwards, against Berger's urging, to the USA, to New York.

Berger claims that it was the only thing the two ever disagreed about, two men who share more or less the same age (Neizvestny, born 1925). Berger thought Neizvestny would be better recognized elsewhere, perhaps in Paris or Stockholm, at any rate somewhere in Europe. He said Neizvestny held an idealized image of New York – just as Neizvestny thought Berger held an idealized image of the USSR! As it transpired, Neizvestny became enormously successful in the US: a big studio in SoHo, a large house in Shelter Island, accolades and commissions almost everywhere, projects in France, Egypt, Israel (Neizvestny is half-Jewish), the Vatican and Sweden, as well as in his native Russia; Gorbachev and Yeltsin both offered him senior positions in the Russian Ministry of Culture; Neizvestny turned each man down. (After a seventeen-year hiatus in meeting, Berger and Neizvestny were dramatically reunited in March 1993, at Annemasse station near Berger's home. The moment was captured, live and unrehearsed, during the filming of *A Telling Eye*, Mike Dibb's documentary on Berger, which aired on BBC TV in 1994. Photographer Jean Mohr was also present to immortalize the historic reencounter.[5])

Berger considered Neizvestny's art important. Neizvestny is a pioneer of revolutionary art and consciousness. He stood as a libertarian Marxist who defied the official Marxist line. The dialectic his art incarnates, particularly vis-à-vis the Soviet state, the dialectic Neizvestny incarnates in himself, reveals for Berger the dialectic between *art* and *revolution*, the needs that art answers, has to answer; it reveals the way Marxist art should – like Sassall's medicine – become an aid to increasing self-consciousness rather than a crude guide to action. Neizvestny's best art, Berger says, demonstrates a Marxist viewpoint *through* it not *in* it. (It is a lesson for any aspiring Marxist artist or writer.)

Art and Revolution, Berger admits, is still the only book he ever wrote because somebody asked him to. That somebody was Neizvestny himself. Neizvestny thought Berger could help 'publicize' his art, bring it to Western eyes, emphasize the struggles of the communist artist to free himself (or herself) from the fetters of Communist Party dogma, from its apparatchiki, from its unfortunate thought-policing. The purpose of Neizvestny's art

Reunited with Ernst Neizvestny.

is not to condone the bureaucratic line, to eulogize it through patriotic socialist realism; neither is it to falsely iron out or deny the nation's ambiguities: rather it is, as Berger says, 'to confine and define the totality in which [these contradictions] exist'.

Neizvestny never flinched from tackling those contradictions, from confronting them head on, usually uncompromisingly. On 1 December 1962 he even confronted Nikita Khrushchev, the USSR's head of state, the First Secretary of the Soviet Communist Party, boss of global communism. It happened at an exhibition organized by the avant-garde Moscow Union of Artists; Neizvestny's offering was denounced as nihilistic. Why do you disfigure the faces of the Soviet people? Khrushchev wondered. At the gallery, Khrushchev exploded with fury, laying into what he saw, calling the exhibits 'dog shit'. Surrounding Khrushchev was a hack entourage who seized Neizvestny and accused him of being a petty crook and 'homosexual'. The bullish sculptor, sometimes known as the 'Centaur', freed himself and retorted: 'If you could find me a girl here and now – I think I should be able to show you.' To which Khrushchev laughed and lightened up.

Then he asked Neizvestny, 'What do you think of art produced under Stalin?' 'I think it was rotten', Neizvestny said, 'and the same kind of artists are still deceiving you.' 'The methods Stalin used were wrong', the head of state admitted, 'but the art itself wasn't.' Neizvestny countered: 'I do not know how, as Marxists, we can think like that. The methods Stalin used served the cult of personality and this became the content of the art he allowed. Therefore the art was rotten too.'

So it went for about an hour, until finally, upon parting, Khrush - chev turned to Neizvestny and said: 'You're the kind of man I like. But there's an angel and a devil in you. If this angel wins, we can get along together. If it's the devil who wins, we shall destroy you.' (In an ironic and touching coda to the confrontation, Khrushchev, in his will, requested that Neizvestny design his headstone;

Neizvestny's sculptured tomb can be seen today at Khrushchev's final resting place, in Moscow's Novodevichi Cemetery.)

When Berger wrote *Art and Revolution* Neizvestny worked semi-clandestinely in a cramped, disused shop in the centre of Moscow; canvases, plaster casts, drawings, huge bronze models and mounds of plasticine were crowded together like goods in a railway wagon. Neizvestny wasn't an 'official' artist so he had to buy his bronze on the black market or else ferret it out from scrap heaps. His studio was badly lit and when he worked he relied more on his fingertips, on touch, than on his eyes. In order to help him begin a new sculpture neighbours down the street came to help Neizvestny move or dismantle an existing piece.

Like a Dostoevskian underground man Neizvestny was discreet in his comings and goings, and forced to live marginally. His private passions, his cravings for contrast and contradictions, however, always bore a public cast. His sculptures, he said, still says, are for the common people, for crowds, for public display and public debate. He was not sure if his political vision drew him to art or if his art stimulated his political vision. What is more certain is how each aspect of his personal and political self gets reflected in every object he creates. Whether in sculptures like *The Prophet* or *Effort*, or in drawings like the astonishing long, circular, 28-panel drawing *Strange Births*, Neizvestny's art, Berger says, 'begins with an insatiable curiosity about the body'. Like the late Dr Sassall Neizvestny is not concerned with the body's beauty 'but with its workings, its power, its resistance, its limits and its mysteries'.

Strange Births is Berger's name for Neizvestny's epic vision of life born in his own mind – what he has seen and lived, what he has feared and hoped for – a remarkable vision of heaven and hell after Dante's *Inferno*. Yet in Neizvestny the division between heaven and hell, as it advances spirally, as it orbits step by step, frame by frame, metre by metre, is not perhaps so neat. At the beginning of *Strange Births* there is a self-portrait of Neizvestny himself, a sort of death mask, which leads us into a world of damaged bodies, of people who at birth seem bound for tragedy; and yet these are bodies that are still *alive*, that still struggle to *live*.

Strange Births forms the centrepiece of Berger's 1969 *Monitor* documentary, 'An Artist in Moscow', brilliantly directed by Hungarian émigré Robert Vas, who committed suicide in 1978 at the age of 47. Vas had quit Hungary in 1956, and the *Monitor* documentary expressed his own existential and political ambivalences, mimicking the very same drama and emotional forces that spun round in Vas's own head: with images of war and Bartók's music synchronizing with extraordinary intensity, the film is nothing short of a mini-masterpiece, a mini-miracle.

A young, debonair Berger, sporting a goatee beard (without moustache) and suit and tie, puts himself in the centre of Neizvestny's mesmerizing creation, discoursing over Bartók on Neizvestny's essential concern for the human body. Bodies are incomplete, adapt, age, change, are overwhelmed by extraneous forces; and yet somehow they overcome, we somehow overcome. (We also lose sometimes, too, as Vas had.) Here Berger's take on *Strange Births* rings out like Bob Dylan's take on life: he who isn't busy being born is busy dying. To this extent, the Neizvestny body is a body that is *becoming*, a body that continues to survive, that clings on through sheer will, through courage, through obstinacy. That is how it offsets victimhood, how it resists victimization. 'The courage of a people or a class', Berger writes near the end of *Art and Revolution*, revealing something of his own existentialism, 'isn't proved by their risking their entire existence: on the contrary, it is proved by their endurance and their determination to survive.'[6]

Neizvestny's art of endurance finds its practical counterpart, Berger thinks, in Latin American revolutionary movements, epitomized by the likes of Che Guevara and guerilla leaders in Guatemala. Yet here, he says, this will to survive expresses an endurance changed from a passive to an *active* one. And 'it applies

With Neizvestny, 'To Friendship!'

no longer to an individual form of stoicism', he says, 'but to a collective determination to survive and to attain the conditions of living in freedom.' All of this, of course, is but a short step away from Mexico's Chiapas jungle, and from the revolutionary endurance of the Zapatistas, voiced by their charismatic insurgent leader, a black ski-masked Subcomandante Marcos, who keeps his face covered for as long as it takes, until it is no longer necessary to wear a disguise, until the threats are over, until it is safe to expose himself, until his 'nakedness' renders him free not fair game.

'Why hide your face?' a journalist once asked Marcos, just after the Zapatista National Liberation Army (ZNLA) had captured 38 key municipalities in Mexico's southernmost state in January 1994, declaring them an autonomous zone outside national and international systems of 'free' trade. 'What are you afraid to show?' the journalist wondered. *El sup* thinks of removing his mask yet suddenly the people cry 'No, no, no!' So the mask stays and the allure persists; an icon is made: behind the mask Marcos does away with his own self and creates another self, the non-self of the everyman and everywoman in revolt against the neoliberal order.

Berger says the incoherence before us today is a New World Order that Marcos labels a 'Fourth World War'. (The Third World War was the so-called Cold War.) The Fourth World War, says Marcos, is 'being conducted between major financial centres in theatres of war that are global in scale and with a level of intensity that is fierce and constant'. Yet this apparent infallibility comes up hard against the stubborn disobedience of a magical reality. Everywhere, Marcos says – in Chiapas and beyond – the full pockets of the financiers meet 'pockets of resistance' of all different shapes and sizes, and of different colours. 'Their sole common point', says Marcos, 'is a desire to resist the New World Order and the crime against humanity that is represented by this Fourth World War.'[7]

Marcos's remarkable essay inspired Berger's collection of essays *The Shape of a Pocket* (2001). Of that book, Berger says: 'I've never written a book with a greater sense of urgency.' 'A pocket is formed', he says,

> when two or more people come together in agreement . . .
> The people coming together [here] are the reader, me and
> those the essays are about – Rembrandt, Palaeolithic cave
> painters, a Romanian peasant, ancient Egyptians, an expert
> in the loneliness of certain hotel bedrooms, dogs at dusk,
> a man in a radio station. And unexpectedly, our exchanges
> strengthen each of us in our conviction that what is happening
> to the world today is wrong, and that what is often said about
> it is a lie.

During the mid-1990s Berger corresponded with the Zapatista insurgent, our very own postmodern Che Guevara. Letters of immense lyrical beauty and intense political passion flowed between the French countryside and Chiapas bush: 'This year', Berger wrote Marcos from Quincy, 'spring came out into the open on April 12th and I'll tell you why . . .

> There were two herons circling with slow wing-beats. They had come back. They were low enough for me to see the black feathers like ribbons which trail from their ears. They were cautiously surveying their terrain together. Yet what caught my breath, Marcos, was the leisure, the ease with which they were doing this. In that leisure there was a momentary yet supreme confidence and sense of belonging. Slowly they circled the place as if they were surveying their own lives to which they had come home. And this made me think of you in Chiapas and of your struggle to restore what has been stolen.[8]

'What is the relationship between the slow beating of the wings of the heron', Marcos later asks Berger, 'with the hovering eagle over a serpent?'

> There were hundreds of them. 'Thousands', says Lieutenant Ricardo, a Tzeltal insurgent who sometimes has a propensity to exaggerate. 'Millions', says Gladys who, despite being twelve years old (or precisely because of it) does not want to be left out. 'They come every year', says grandfather while the small flashes of white hover above the village, and maybe disappear towards the east? Are they coming or going? Are they your herons, Mr Berger? A winged reminder? Or a greeting filled with premonition? A fluttering of wings of something that resists death? . . . For this system which concentrates wealth and power and distributes death and poverty, the *campesinos*, the indigenous, do not fit in the plans and projects. They have to be got rid of, just like the herons . . . and the eagles . . . have

to be got rid of . . . It has to do with the eagle and the heron, the European *campesino* who is resisting being absorbed and the Latin American indigenous who is rebelling against genocide . . . And it has to do with, I reiterate and salute it in this way, the letters that come from you to us, and those that, with these lines, bring you these words: the eagle received the message, he understood the approach of the hesitant flight of the heron. And there below, the serpent trembles and fears the morning.[9]

In December 2007 Berger and Marcos finally met face to face, speaking on the same podium; the heron took his slow-beating winged flight (even though he hates flying!), greeting the *campesino* eagle in the bush. The occasion was an International Colloquium in the Chiapas town of San Cristóbal de las Casas, paying homage to the French anthropologist and longtime champion of indigenous peoples Andrés Aubry, who was killed nearby in a car accident the previous September. Berger had seen, there and then, a different political vocabulary getting uttered. The Zapatistas, he later put it in *Le blaireau et le roi*, 'have re-injected a certain poetics into politics. They've changed the syntax of political discourse.' Since 1996 Marcos and his band of insurgents have renounced armed struggle. Yet if attacked, if ever threatened by firepower, they are more than prepared to defend themselves with arms.

'I have never met a group of people so calm', Berger says, reflecting upon his Chiapas visit. 'Calm with the certitude of rejecting all certitudes. It gives them an extraordinary tranquility, radically opposed to despair.' One illustration of this calm was meeting Marcos:

Before I went to his home, a wooden cabin, I'd imagined all sorts of questions to ask him. We embraced. He led me to his room, the size of a small workshop. I had the impression that we'd known each other for a long time; we weren't intimate:

we were familiar. Somehow there was no urgency to talk, not even about important things. Perhaps it was the calm, the certitude of no certitude, that meant there was little need to discuss the global situation.

Behind the black mask, under that large nose, Berger had heard a mouth and larynx silently speak about hope, about resistance, about survival, about strange births to come. So, too, was Marcos a fortunate man, a free man, an enduring artist . . .

Marcos' silent voice speaks volumes about Berger's own firebrand Marxism, a Marxism that shifts the ballast away from critique to affirmation, to something *positive*, to a creative autono - mous alternative. For Berger the Zapatista's modus operandi is educative for all *résistants*, not least because it pivots around the notion of *action* wedded to *critique*: the struggle for autonomy is the prime mover of their uprising; resistance has since become the rearguard manoeuvring necessary to defend this autonomy. The ordering is important: *affirmation* and then *resistance*. You struggle for what you want, try to make it work, achieve it though believing in yourself, through sheer will – whether in art, medicine or politics – and then you dig in. And through endurance, through collective obstinacy, you struggle on, you hold on with others doing likewise. Together you resist. This is how solidarity is formulated, how great art is fashioned, how people are 'cured'.

This is what a Bergerian philosophy of life, art and politics equally constitutes: poetic as well as pragmatic, a Marxism somehow beyond time. Beyond time, because it is a Marxism in which liberty is non-negotiable, is a transhistorical human *condition*. Liberty, we might say, is eternal: there is neither when nor before nor after here, only *now*. 'It is not something awaiting us', Berger says, 'but something we encounter during those brief yet timeless moments when everything accommodates everything and no exchange is inadequate.'[10]

7

About Time and Space

'Sometimes, I'd like to write a book/ A book all about time/ About how it doesn't exist,/ How the past and the future/ Are one continuous present.'
Yevgeny Vinokurov

'So time doesn't count and place does? I asked again. It's not any place, John, it's a meeting place.'
Berger and his mother, cited in *Here is Where We Meet*

Once upon a time a farmer was on his way to the Italian market town of Biella. The weather was so foul that it was nigh impossible to pass the roads. But the farmer had important business. And in the face of the driving rain, he pushed on regardless. After a while, he met an old man who said, 'A good day to you! Where are you going, my good man, in such a hurry?'

'To Biella', replied the farmer, without slowing down.

'You might at least say "God willing".'

The farmer stopped, looked the old man in the eye, and snapped, 'God willing, I'm on the way to Biella. But even if God isn't willing, I still have to go there all the same.'

Now it just so happened that the old man was God. 'In that case', he said, 'you'll go to Biella in seven years.' 'In the meantime, jump into this pond and stay there for seven years.'

Suddenly, the farmer changed into a frog and leapt into the pond.

Seven years went by. The farmer came out of the pond, turned back into a man, clapped his hat on his head, and set off once more for the market.

After a short distance, he met the same old man. 'And where are you going today, my good man?'

'To Biella.'

'You might say, "God willing".'

'If God wills it, fine. If not, I know what's going to happen and I'll jump into the pond of my own free will!'

'Those Stubborn Souls', summarized above, appears in Italo Calvino's edited collection *Italian Folktales*. The tale was read aloud by Berger in the first of a series of television programmes devised and directed by Mike Dibb and Chris Rawlence, produced for Channel 4, called 'About Time' (1984). It was about time somebody did something about time; so here was Berger again, in 'Once Upon a Time', in front of the camera in episode One, attired in a country plaid shirt, reading and telling stories, enigmatic stories, compellingly read stories about our longstanding desire to invent strategies to outwit time. With deceptive simplicity – a no-frills approach unimaginable in today's era of spectacle television – we hear of farmers who uphold their free will, come what may, and romantic young men who want to find the magical kingdom where people live not for 300 years nor for 400: they want to find that magical place where nobody *ever* dies.

In 'About Time', Berger tells stories about those who want to defy the inexorability of time, those who want to offset death. Their desire – our desire – is nothing less than a desire for *immortality*, even if they (we) know immortality is folly, is a silly fairy tale, a 'once upon a time . . .'. Yet in knowing it is only a fairy tale, living out this fairy tale, dreaming and telling fairy tales, remembering the past and re-imagining the future, we have already begun to discover our own immortality; we have already begun to *deconstruct* linear

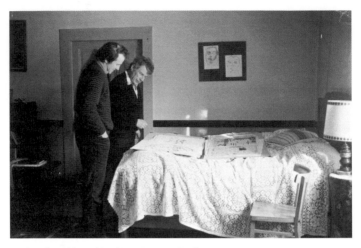

With Mike Dibb, making 'Once Upon a Time'.

time, to take it apart at the seams. It is the soul which pierces time, says Berger; people go on loving each other long after one partner has died, long after their body ceases to be in time. In remembering, in dreaming, in entering a story, tellers and listeners find joint communion in an eternal present.

In Western culture our chief principle of time is linear, measured time, GMT and industrial time, a synchronized time that has overwhelmed other experiences of time; we have lost something of ourselves in the process, Berger thinks. Modern men and women have become victims of their own time-terror, of their own time-positivism. We have introduced an abstract time, a historical time reduced to quantification, to hours and minutes and seconds, to days and months and years. Hours and minutes are relatively recent inventions; they only tell the time we have conceived for ourselves. 'Only when time is unilinear', Berger warns, 'does the foreseeing of a future event or the pre-existence of a destiny imply determinism, and thus a crucial loss of freedom. If there is a plurality of times, or if time is cyclic, then prophesy and destiny can coexist with a freedom of choice.' Only in cyclic time can farmers *choose* to become frogs.[1]

About Time gives a fascinating insider glimpse of Berger's Haute-Savoie daily life, of its cyclic temporality punctuated by seasonality, by the rhythms of nature, by harvests and haymaking, by festivals and remembrance, an elemental time that Berger personally embraces. He sometimes tells his stories in his own kitchen; we see him lighting his old wood-burning stove; he dreams lonely dreams in his own outhouse; we feel the Alpine moods, the freezing snow, the spring thaw, smell piled-up wood, glimpse seeds quietly pushing up through damp mountain earth, searching for the first glimmers of warm sunshine. We hear a deep rural song, a hollow sleepiness that's fecund. Old barns nd rusty ploughs, the gentle sounds of the village accordion and Jew's harp resound across dramatic *alpage* and luminous jagged peaks. 'We spent ten deep winter days filming with John', Chris Rawlence recalls,

> at his house in Mieussy. The blanket of snow outside heightened our sense of being archetypal listeners, gathered round the

Sketching Beverly in 'Once Upon a Time'.

hearth of the storyteller at the dead time of year. In fact, the stories that John told for the film were written and delivered on the hoof – a just-in-time approach to filmmaking that suited Mike's [Dibb] improvisatory approach. Stories.

Berger is not lamenting lost time, time going backwards, a return to peasant time. Although he acknowledges there is much to learn here, recognizing that the peasant clock has been actively annihilated, wiped out by other dictates of time, Berger's wish is to affirm other loci of time, other temporal coordinates for conditioning life on earth, for inspiring collective resistance, for ensuring planetary survival. Time can be lived differently, he says, ought to be lived differently. Fairy tales cast political spells, can even bewitch the 'realist' time-narrative of Power. For nowadays, he suggests, the dominance of uniform, abstract time has become a law unto itself – with detrimental consequences for history as well as geography. In its most modern manifestation, in its most logical, brutalized and stripped-down form, it has engendered an unprecedented awareness of time: *digital time.*

According to this clock, a singular, empty present presides, an LCD time in which all history and memory, all past and future have been evacuated, ripped off and plundered by digital time. Digital time, Berger says, continues forever uninterrupted through day and night, through the seasons, through birth and death. Onward it travels, brooking no dissent. It is the air-conditioned nightmare of a strip mall that never closes, a fake smile and a pinstripe on the job, the ordered routine of organization men. It is as indifferent to particularity and quality as money, similarly lacking specific gravity: only the present is weight-bearing. It contrasts to the cyclical time of nature, of cold and warmth, of presence and feeling, of pain, of dreams and fairy tales, of the gratitude of watching donkeys graze on a mountain meadow. Digital time knows only a single vertical column of ones and zeros, of cash flows and Dow indices. Time is money, the old adage goes; 'the economy of time', says Marx in his *Grundrisse*, 'to this all economy ultimately reduces itself'. Any other moment, any little meanwhile that falls in between, non-money-making time, is time deemed a dead moment, a waste of time, an empty instant off-line.

Nothing surrounds this verticality, this vertical digital time, except absence. No *whereabouts* can be found or established, Berger says. Journeys no longer have a specific content of a *destination*. Destination has lost its territory of experience. We see territories of experience, he says, in, for example, the poetry of Emily Dickinson, just as we see desolate spaces in Lars Von Trier's film *Dogville*. Here, where people are left stranded, cut off from the past, insulated from the future, there is a present without *presentness*. Following signs in airport lounges, at supermarket checkouts, on motorways, on mobile phones, will never lead to a destination. When we arrive we realize we are not in the place indicated by the signs we followed; neither do we know what time it is. And nobody can give us directions, because neither they nor we know what to ask for. All words and language are rendered vacant. All trace of eternity, those timeless moments when everything accommodates everything else, has been erased from daily life.

Vertical digital time is straight and goes either up or down. It judges by numbers, by cost-benefit charts, by GDPs and growth projections, by 'rational' objective Truth. Within its verticality there is little room for anything mysterious, for anything *horizontal*, for alternative clocks ticking to other beats. Science keeps digital time in check. Science has become something of a metronome for digital time, its handmaiden, or at least its midwife. On the question of time, says Berger, science is now bound to be solipsist. The problem of time thus boils down to a problem of choice – or lack of it. In horizontal time, by contrast, there are other choices, differ-ent undulations, random dips in the road, curves and bends and junctions, alleyways and back roads, some of which are unpaved and full of mud. In horizontal time there are unforeseen twists and gravitational pulls that *warp* time, that make it relative not absolute, elliptical rather than numerical.

To some extent Berger's own clock is synchronized more to animal time. For animals, he says, time is an unbroken, continuous present that is *really* present; animals have a confidence that sees time as if it is laid out as space. Animals have little sense of time as we humans understand it. They wait, of course, wait patiently to be fed; but this patience, Berger says, is not quite what it seems to be. Time, insofar as it is experienced at all by animals, is experienced more like space. All animals' senses alert them to what is happening *here* and *there*, rather than today or tomorrow. Animals can be frightened, they can experience pleasure and pain, but they have no anxiety about tomorrow. So they need no philosophy of time, no abstract, vertical time. Berger's time warp is likewise found in horizontal space, in time laid out as if it is sensed here and there, a space where a vertical line crisscrosses a horizontal line.

But this vertical line does not imply digital time; it is a path leading both upwards towards the sky and downwards towards the underworld, to a place where the past lies buried, even if it is never quite dead. The horizontal line, meanwhile, represents all possible roads across the globe, trails towards other places. Where these two lines meet – the vertical and the horizontal – is a kind of reassurance, something Berger suggests we might call *home*, a spot that is at once a starting point and a returning point, a Being- as well as Becoming-in-the-world. Thus to lose those coordinates means to be *displaced*, to be lost in time and space, directed by a compass and a clock that only adds to one's anguish, to one's feeling of vertigo. Under neoliberal capitalism, no longer are there any fixed points as bearings: up is only timeless time, outwards and across is only a plane of pure distance.

Signposts, billboards and digital screens, insists Berger, will never locate the heres and theres that make human encounters possible, that make them meaningful and sustainable. It is in Bergerian heres and theres that the dead commune with the living, where they reach out across the black divide, through the flames; history is kept alive in space and animal time moos in its old barn. 'So time doesn't count and place does?' Berger wonders, teasing his late mother in *Here is Where We Meet* (2005). 'It's not any place, John', she replies, 'it's a meeting place . . . Everything in life, John, is a question of drawing a line, and you have to decide for yourself where to draw it.'[2]

In *Here is Where We Meet*, published 30 years on from *About Time*, time once again gets laid out as space. Eight short stories converge (and diverge) in this suggestively titled book, Berger's most surrealist and autobiographical trip to date, his exquisite corpse, a collection that is as tender as the night. Berger floats in and out of a dreamy, subliminal zone where space and time lose all recognized empirical moorings, and where living landscapes – in Lisbon, Geneva, London, Madrid, Kraków, the Ardèche – harbour furtive afterlives. Buried pasts become sacred presents in which roam his mother and old teachers, former lovers and dear friends, all long departed but seemingly never, ever forgotten; personal time melds with grand historical time; a blind Borges communes with a limping Rosa Luxemburg; Rembrandt's *Polish Rider* with Cro-Magnon cave paintings; rivers literally thousands of miles apart merge into one torrent of imagination; the boy Berger watches an aged John make sorrel soup while dreaming of wild Polish country weddings and his father's trench warfare. Past encounters offer Berger a special Proustian key for unlocking the future, for conveying his quantum curiosity. 'The number of lives that enter any one life is', he says, 'incalculable.'

Rendezvousing with his dead mother in Lisbon – 'a city of endurance, unanswerable questions and pet names' – she reminds him: 'everything begins with a death.' 'Isn't the beginning a birth?' he queries. 'That's the common error, and you fell into the trap as I thought you would!' 'The births happened precisely because they offered a chance of repairing some of what was damaged from the beginning, after the death. That's why we are here, John, to repair . . . to repair a little of what was broken.' 'Why did you never read any of my books?' he wonders. 'All my books have been about you.' 'They were about everything in the world but me! I've had to wait until now, until you are an old man in Lisboa, for you to be writing this very short story about me.' You can't afford to make a mistake anymore, she scolds her wayward son, about whether you're lying or whether you're trying to tell the truth.

Old man Berger, hesitantly and insecurely, greets Maman across a golden curtain of sunlight and water. Before her, like all adult men, he remains a little boy. Without a mother, without those friends and mentors whom he has outlived or outgrown, he is alone: *Here is Where We Meet* is an orphan form, a book born out of a sense of loneliness, perhaps a recognition of Berger's own mortality, his irreconcilable homesickness, his yearning to be at home everywhere. His presence unnerves, unnerves because of its strange invisibility: he is there on his motorbike, but he is not there, he sees but can never quite be seen. In fact Berger sees things mere mortals cannot, like a trenchcoated Bruno Ganz from Wim Wenders's *Wings of Desire*, an unlikely angel, coursing around a universe that is both monochrome and in colour; colour for celebrations, for remembering the bride's dress; monochrome for Rosa's dark locks, for the grey history of her smashed-in head, her lifeless body fished out of the Landwehr Canal.

In speaking of death the angel Berger reminds us of the every-day joys of life at its most simplest, of experience most rooted and immediate, of slicing leeks and savouring beer, of plum brandy and newborn kids, of first snow and nightjars, of motor-cycle boots and fried potatoes. Berger really notices things, really knows how to look, how to hear and feel little details around him. And he remembers. His pen flows as Walter Benjamin's flowed in

Naples or in Berlin, chronicling montages, glimpses and motifs. Autobiography, Benjamin said, has a lot to do with time, with sequence, with 'the continuous flow of life'; but Benjamin's concern was with something different, with discontinuities and moments: he remembered only *spaces*. Ditto Berger, who writes as evocatively about bustling public squares as he does about darkened, deserted forests.

He has a painter's gift – unsurprisingly for an ex-painter – for sketching with words colours and sensations, for evoking tonalities and moods of landscapes that literally blossom with childlike wonderment, with an almost naive purity of a romantic poet; they are realities invented rather than discovered: 'it is pointless', he says in one Geneva *rencontre*, 'to search in the places where people are instructed to look. Sense is only found in secrets.' Perhaps the secret of *Here is Where We Meet*, Berger's secret, is not found in people at all but in *places*, in elemental places, meeting places, spaces in which humans and animals, vegetables and minerals are really all just attributes of one Spinozan substance.

The concept of place – the idea of meeting places – is every-where in Berger's oeuvre, everywhere in Berger's imagination, everywhere in his politics. It is there in Quincy, there as he rides his motorbike, and it is there in his head and between the lines. 'Questions of geography', 'questions of place', a 'sense of place', the 'place of painting', 'meeting places' – keeping rendezvouses (in which vertical and horizontal time and space intersect) – are the lifeblood of Berger the man, the artist, and the concerned citizen. A place, he reminds us, is more than an arena and more than a mere trace on a map. A place implies a *presence* not an absence, a fullness and connectivity; it implies something *alive*, the consequence of an action and an activity.

It is perhaps more adequately defined existentially than materially. A place is the opposite of empty space, the opposite of something artificial and inert, of something prefabricated and self-consciously manufactured, of a decoration or a representation. Bergerian places are entities as well as flows, invisible as well as visible categories, bounded sites in which certain properties are momentarily instantiated; almost always those instances, even if they endure for centuries, are subject to negotiation: they are never cast in stone even if they're sometimes demarcated by stone. A place can offer shelter, warmth, protection, be a hearth in a heartless (and heartless) world, a site of resistance, a starting point for survival. Yet places can also imprison, condemn, prevent, keep people in as well as out.

The relationship between place and space, and the whole question of geography in our globalized, neoliberal age, in our post-9/11 reality, has more and more preoccupied an ageing Berger. On the one hand, as a writer, he knows how poems can be places, can become dwelling places, sites one can enter, *visit* as well as read; there, words act like stones of some delicate habitation, enveloping you, comforting you. Nonetheless, for Berger the politico, words alone have their limitations: here and there one needs to put verse into action, meld artistry with activism.

Over recent decades curious things have happened to our urban and rural spaces. Spaces where people could once wander and linger, in public and in common, meeting places in which people could keep rendezvouses, have steadily been transmogrified into spick and span privatized zones whose clients are exclusively the well-heeled. Once shabby yet decent mixed neighbourhoods have become homogenized and gentrified, unaffordable for former occupants, unaffordable for most people apart from the already rich who all seem to look the same, dress the same, consume the same. Our urban spaces have become banal playgrounds for real estate corporations and financial institutions, for sleek executives and gawking tourists, for upscale services and the highest bidder. Post-industrial enclaves now displace people spatially while they reshape people temporally, fostering insecure and underpaid work and overworked workers, frequently migrant workers, who all need several jobs to pay the bills. A denial of space here equates to a pilfering of time, to a widening disjuncture between where people live, or where they can afford to live, and where they can still find a job, to the hours wasted journeying in log-jammed traffic or doing mammoth hikes, frequently on foot in the developing world.

Just as ordinary people are exploited and downsized at work, so too are they now exploited and downsized where they live. Physical removal from decent paying jobs, with decent contracts, with decent benefits, has been 'complemented' by their physical removal from decent neighbourhoods, from homes and hometowns with once-decent services and affordable rents. Liberalism extracted surplus value by exploiting at the global workplace; neoliberalism now extracts its cut by dispossessing people in the global living space, by sequestering the commons, by re-appropriating the centres of our cities at the same time as it pauperizes our most 'productive' rural land. Just as capitalism prospers from *abstract labour* at the workplace, so it grows and flourishes through the production of *abstract space*, through its office blocks and luxury apartments, its global markets and factory agriculture; and where abstract space reigns few secrets lurk – save insider trading and money laundering.

Twenty-first-century political struggles will, Berger thinks, be above all territorial struggles, struggles to reclaim space, to establish new senses of place, new meeting places wherein worldwide solidarity transcends modern homelessness. Today's contested terrain and central node of analysis are not factories as such, but abandoned rural spaces and teeming urban streets, shantytowns and nowherevilles the world over, localities now deemed redundant in the dumpster culture of world market life. As Berger sees it, places are sites of capital accumulation and domination on the one side, and of organized solidarity and revolt on the other. Thus a place's double-edged nature, its inexorable dialectic, its humane hope as well as its genocidal threat: never underestimate the power of geography. The adage goes for both the dispossessed global poor and the empowered transnational elite.

The metanarrative of the world is no longer a straight story sequentially unfolding in time, despite what its pundits claim. There is no metanarrative. Our mode of narration has fundamentally changed, says Berger. Stories are now continually traversed *laterally*, by an infinite number of storylines that bisect the straight-line story, disrupting it, creating simultaneity and extension, particularity and fragmentation. The reasons why are numerous and complex: high-tech means of communication, market integration, globalization, concurrent centralization and decentralization of power, the widening scale of exploitation, the indivisibility of life on the planet, and so on, and so on. All of these factors play their decisive part. As such 'prophesy', says Berger,

> now involves a geographical rather than historical projection; it is space not time that hides consequences from us. To prophesize today it is only necessary to know men as they are throughout the whole world in all their inequality. Any contemporary narrative which ignores the urgency of this dimension is incomplete.[3]

'The in-ex-or-ab-le hell of geography', one of the characters screams, cathartically, in Berger and Nella Bielski's play *A Question of Geography*. When the French National Theatre of Marseille first performed the play in 1985, followed by the Royal Shakespeare Company of Stratford-upon-Avon in 1987, its theme seemed quaint and rather outmoded: after all, the ghosts of the Gulag were soon about to be exorcized under glasnost and perestroika. These days the Gulag no longer exists – excepting perhaps Guantánamo Bay. Yet millions of people continue to labour under conditions that are not very different. What has changed, Berger says, is the forensic logic applied to workers and criminals.

A Question of Geography is not a great play; it is much better seen than read. One is constantly aware that something tendentious is unfolding, that the handful of characters condemned to permanent exile for 'Article 58' crimes against the Soviet state, not long after Stalin's death, are mouthpieces for transmitting some deeper existential point, and that it is this point which drives their actions, promotes their words. Where the play just about pulls it off is in the fact that this existential point is never peddled in a heavy-handed way; a hoping humanity is always transmitted subtly and honestly.

The ostensible geography in question is the geography of the vast *taïga* region of Magadan, the capital of the *Gulag*, the acronym for the USSR's State Authority for Camps. The whole region is cut off from the rest of the country by mountains and frozen Arctic tundra. The only way in is by air or boat. Magadan is not an island in the strict sense of the term, but to live there is to be exiled offshore, far away from anything, far from 'mainland' Russia. Thus the feeling of physical isolation is part of the dread zone of Magadan's topography.

Yet the *real* question of geography that concerns Berger and Bielski is less vast in its physicality, more enclosed in its hermetic scale. Indeed, it is there where the biggest threats reside, where the walls close in the narrowest, where the overbearing sense of permanent surveillance creates claustrophobia within the self, within each inmate, who in time begins to internalize their own culpability of internment. Somehow 'Bruises' are everywhere, those Zone administrators, the designated guards and official warders, all of whom might come knocking at your door any time of the day or night. The question of Gulag geography is forever duplicitous. Never is anything more two-faced, interior as well as exterior: the white frozen fog chills the spirit as well as the body.

At the same time, precisely because these threats are closer to home, less remote in their geographical scale, the more contestable they are, the more apt to be subverted at the level of daily life.

Bruises guard distant and invisible ideological interests, interests of distant and invisible masters; yet inmates like Dacha and Ernst and Gricha fight for something vitally nearer to them, for themselves, for their own Being, and learn, ever so slowly, ever so painfully, how to adapt on their own terms the rules of the authority's game. Even in a cell, even in minus 40-degree temperatures, even with only 400 grams of bread a day, geography is always and everywhere negotiated terrain.

This seems to be Berger and Bielski's profounder hope against hope, their mischievous response to the spatial question they pose. What is the potential space of choice? What are its limits? How far can you push outwards those spatial limits, transcend those limits? 'Everything outside forbids a choice', Ernst says. 'The choices we make are inside.' 'You empty a wheelbarrow full of rock', he adds, illustrating the lesson he is giving to the teenage boy Sacha.

> About pushing the barrow to the dump you have no choice. Now it's empty you have a choice. You can walk your barrow back just like you came, or – if you're clever, and survival makes you clever – you push it back like this, almost upright. If you choose the second way you give your shoulders a rest. If you are a Zek [prisoner] and you become a team leader, you have the choice of playing at being a screw, or of never forgetting that you are a Zek.

This principle of choice presumably still applies, though today the inmates wear different fatigues. And what constitutes the question of the geography of incarceration these days has significantly changed its spots. 'During the Gulag', Berger says, reflecting more recently on the transformed question of the geography of incarceration, 'political prisoners, categorized as criminals, were reduced to slave-labourers. Today millions of brutally exploited workers are being reduced to the status of criminals.' Once, the Gulag equation meant 'criminal = slave labourer'. Now, neoliberalism has redrafted its remit: 'worker = hidden criminal'. 'The whole drama of global migration', says Berger, 'is expressed in this new formula: those who work are latent criminals. When accused, they are found guilty of trying at all costs to survive.'

Fifteen million Mexicans slip across the US to work without papers each year and are consequently criminalized; a massive concrete wall, 1,200 kilometres in length, stretches across the border, 'virtually' monitored by 1,800 watchtowers, there to keep the migrant workers out.

> Between industrial capitalism, dependent on manufacture and factories, and financial capitalism, dependent on free-market speculation and front office traders, the incarceration area has changed. Speculative financial transactions add up, each day, to 1,300 billion dollars . . . The prison is now as large as the planet and its allotted zones vary and can be termed worksite, refugee camp, shopping mall, periphery, ghetto, office block, favela, suburb. What is essential is that those incarcerated in these zones are fellow prisoners.[4]

Therein lies the figurative image Berger has been searching for. He wants an image, he says, that can serve as a 'landmark' for understanding the contemporary age, a reference point that can be shared, confronted. 'The landmark I've found is that of prison. Nothing less. Across the planet we are living in a prison.' Importantly, this is not a metaphor: the imprisonment is real. Penitentiaries still exist and are increasingly being built to keep people in. Yet today's prison serves a different purpose. Today a lot of prison walls are there not to keep prisoners in, in some kind of 'corrective' confinement, but to keep prisoners out, to exclude them, to separate them as other. And those walls may be concrete, cast in stone across borderlands; yet they are also electronically patrolled walls, interrogating walls, ideological and fearmongering walls that keep 'outsiders' at bay, that fend people off, that banish them to distant hinterlands.

The sense of tyranny has changed because our sense of space and time has changed. What is being lived out now, Berger insists, is new because its relationship with space and time is new. Here, following the thinking of the sociologist Zygmunt Bauman, corporate market forces are at the helm of a reality that's essentially 'extra-territorial', which is to say 'free from territorial constraints – constraints of locality'. Those in control are perpetually remote, serially anonymous, and thus take little account of the territorial and physical consequences of their actions, of their unaccountable boardroom decisions.

This extra-territorial ruling class is shaping out its own digital and virtual core at the epicentre of financial and corporate affairs, 'Haussmannizing' nodes of wealth and information, power and communication from the inside, doing so while it creates a real feudal dependency on the outside, an excluded population who more and more inhabit a vast global *banlieue* in the making – often making it themselves. Controlling and containing this novel situation, keeping in check mass populations – who, remember, consist of consumers as well as producers – is now the task of typically effete national governments: 'The planet is a prison and the obedient governments, whether of right or left, are the herders.'

Our new prison system operates largely thanks to cyberspace and cybertime, offering the market a speed of exchange that is almost instantaneous, shifting commodities around the globe, trading money night and day, speculating on currency rate fluctuations, futures and options, doing it all with an unprecedented velocity, mimicking the turnover rate that Marx projected as every capitalist's wet dream: 'the twinkling of an eye'. By this clock 24 hours is a very long period; and by those spatial coordinates distances in every direction shrink on a frictionless, delocalized, isotropic plain. The net effect is that there is

no place for pain in that velocity; announcements of pain perhaps, but not the suffering of it. Consequently, the human condition is banished, excluded from those operating the system. Earlier, tyrants were pitiless and inaccessible, but they were neighbours who were subject to pain. This is no longer the case, and therein lies the system's probable weakness.

Meanwhile, how to live in this present that forbids cyclical time and spatial particularity? Meanwhile – doesn't all political resistance begin in a *meanwhile*? Berger asks, the time and space of the meanwhile, the moment between the tick, the split-second lapse, the crack in the isotropic surface, a trace of mud, a fairy tale of hope, the strange comings together and solidarities announced *because* of cyberspace, because it produces its own gravediggers – all this signals, hints at, new meeting places getting made and new covert rendezvouses being kept. At these moments and in these spaces, people ignore jailers' talk. What screws say, their shibboleths and mantras, their banalities about freedom and security, about democracy against terrorism, 'repeated and repeated in order to confuse, divide, distract and sedate all fellow prisoners', are no longer meaningful in our meanwhiles; they are untranslatable this side of the Great Wall.

Here prisoners have their own vocabulary, their own argot, their own everyday language. Here words speak a lexicon of dissimula - tion and secrecy, beyond the reach of cyber-jargon, which is created by specialists, by people with power and wealth, by elites profiting from patent and monopoly. On this side of the wall prisoners create their own walls, which offer the shelter of a knowing crowd closing around itself, as if protecting a fugitive. This is the vocab - ulary of the dispossessed: it provokes and riles, is profane and rough and defies authority. It does not lay out a single screen, a solid wall, but is a play of mirrors and lighting, is a secret subversion, because prisoners have found their own idiosyncratic ways to communicate with one another. Inmates now know the power of their own words, recalling always that it's dangerous to speak: sometimes too much, sometimes too little.

Authority has no grasp on this language, or on the words, precisely because authority is extra-territorial. Rulers oversee power but they themselves live tucked away from those they oversee, in their gated communities, or up in the sky, with little sense of what is happening down below, on the street, in the 'hood. 'They have no knowledge of the surrounding earth', says Berger. 'Furthermore, they dismiss such knowledge as superficial, not profound. Only extracted resources count. They cannot listen to the earth. On the ground they are blind. In the local they are lost.' Walls have two sides. Cells now touch other cells like a giant global beehive, and ever so steadily, worker bees are discovering where the honey is. Liberty is slowly being found not outside the walls, Berger says, but in the very depths of the prison, inside the honeycombs. 'Everything outside forbids a choice', Ernst said in *A Question of Geography*. 'The choices we make are inside.'

It is perhaps the only thing that never ever changes with incarceration.

8

Confronting Walls

'That wall/ That wall/ They are shooting our people/ in front of that wall!/ That wall/ there is mobilization in front of that wall . . .'.
Nazim Hikmet, 'The Wall of Imperialism'

'A box of stone/ where the living and the dead move in the dry clay/ like bees captive in a honeycomb in a hive/ and each time the siege tightens/ they go on a flower hunger strike/ and ask the sea to indicate the emergency exit . . .'.
Mahmoud Darwish, 'The Mural'

The world's biggest prison, Berger says, is nowadays the Gaza Strip, in the future state of Palestine, currently in territories occupied by Israel. The West Bank, meanwhile, is the world's largest waiting room, a room in which one awaits this seemingly distant future. The Gaza area is dominated by a giant 8-metre-tall, 210-kilometre-long concrete wall, the so-called 'West Bank Barrier' which runs loosely along the path of the 1949 Jordanian-Israeli armistice 'Green Line', inside the northwestern and western edges of the West Bank. (The Wall will stretch to 640 kilometres once finished.) Israelis label it a 'security fence' or 'anti-terrorist fence', maintaining that it is necessary to protect Israeli civilians from Palestinian terrorism, from suicide bomb attacks; opponents say the wall deviates dramatically from the Green Line and is an illegal attempt to annex Palestinian land under the pretext of Israeli 'security'.

The wall, say critics, is an 'Apartheid Wall' that violates international law and limits Palestinian free movement. Forced checkpoints, road closures, loss of land and problems accessing work and water, medical and educational services, is the net outcome in Palestinian daily life. 'It's difficult to overstate the humanitarian impact of the barrier', the United Nations wrote in a March 2005 report.

> The route inside the West Bank severs communities, people's access to services, livelihoods and religious and cultural amenities. In addition, plans for the Barrier's exact route and crossing points through it are often not fully revealed until days before the construction commences. This has led to considerable anxiety amongst Palestinians about how their future lives will be impacted . . . The land between the Barrier and the Green Line constitutes some of the most fertile in the West Bank.

'The checkpoints function as interior frontiers imposed on the Occupied Territories', Berger himself makes more precise,

> yet they do not resemble any normal frontier post. They are constructed and manned in such a way that everyone who passes is reduced to the status of an unwelcome refugee. Impossible to overestimate the importance for the stranglehold of décor, used as a constant reminder of who are the victors and who should recognize that they are the conquered. Palestinians have to undergo, often several times a day, the humiliation of playing the part of refugees in their own land. Everyone crossing has to walk on foot past the checkpoint, where soldiers, loaded guns at the ready, pick on whoever they wish to 'check'. No vehicles can cross. The traditional road has been destroyed. The new obligatory 'route' has been strewn with boulders,

stones and other minor obstacles. Consequently, all, even the fit, have to hobble across.[1]

Every Palestinian living in occupied territories is compelled to carry an ID card that is either orange or green: orange for urban dwellers, green for those who live in the countryside; each colour has its own restrictions with regard to checkpoint exits and entrances; all information on the ID card is in Hebrew and only the person's name is in Arabic. (Officially Palestinians are known as 'Israeli Arabs'; recently the adjective Palestinian was forbidden.) Every card has a number that Israeli soldiers can tap into their mobile phone; name, address and past record appear; rarely, though, is there a Palestinian family without a member who has done time in an Israeli gaol. 'Yet despite the stored and coded information', Berger says,

> they have nothing to do with identity. They are simply an inventory of stolen facts. True identity can be neither delivered on demand nor stored as mere information. To believe that it can be, is the weakness of all so-called security records kept by oppressors. True identity is something known in one heart and recognized within another. It always contains a secret that no interrogation can reveal. Its secret is its human-beingness.

For a while now, Berger has been a staunch supporter of Palestinian rights and a vociferous advocate of this future state the other side of the wall; he has also been a fierce critic of Israel and the continued barbarity of its Israeli Defense Force (IDF), a de facto army of conquest which, he says, exists to guarantee the continuation of theft of Palestinian land. In 2006 in a letter to *The Guardian* (15 December 2006), he and 93 other signatories from the world of literature and performing arts (including musician Brian Eno, artist Cornelia Parker and writer Arundhati Roy) called for a 'cultural boycott of Israel'. 'The boycott is an active protest against two forms of exclusion', Berger wrote,

> which have persisted, despite many other forms of protest-ations, for over sixty years – for almost three generations. During this period the state of Israel has consistently excluded itself from any international obligation to heed UN resolutions or the judgment of any international court. To date, it has defied 246 Security Council Resolutions! As Nelson Mandela has pointed out, boycott is not a principle, it is a tactic depending upon circumstances. A tactic which allows people, as distinct from their elected but often craven governments, to apply a certain pressure on those wielding power in what they, the boycotters, consider to be an unjust or immoral way. (In white South Africa yesterday and in Israel today, the immorality was, or is being, coded into a form of racist apartheid.)

Over the past decade an ageing Berger has embarked upon his own personal solidarity missions, making several trips to Palestine as gestures of support: in the spring of 2003, in the autumn of 2005 and in December 2008. The last two occasions were *en famille*, with the whole Berger gang travelling together: Beverly and Yves, the latter's partner Sandra, as well as their then three-year-old daughter, Melina, a blonde ray of sunshine who charmed the little Palestinian boys. (There is an amazing photo of grandfather Berger – *Papi* – dressed in his 'wounded red' shirt holding Melina's hand, taken during the autumn 2005 sojourn.[2] They are ambling along a worn dirt track directly underneath the Israeli Wall. The little girl, in her innocent white dress, seems to make the barrier's scale look even more immense and daunting, even more brutal, even more unforgivable for the next generation. Yet somehow the scene evokes 'undefeated despair'; the wall is adorned with graffiti and splattered high above is the message: 'TO EXIST IS TO RESIST'.)

John and Melina at the West Bank wall.

In Ramallah Berger and Yves did a series of art workshops
with young Palestinian artists (and kids) at the Khalil Sakakini
Cultural Center, a space that encourages new talents expressive
of Palestinian cultural heritage and collective memory. The
interchange between John, Yves and the participants operated
largely at the practical level, and everybody learned from one
another. How can one judge the value of a work of art? Berger
queried. When is it finished? How can it be exposed to critique
and discussion? Art, he said, is never a predetermined activity
but necessarily involves exploration and experimentation.
It means mistakes and problem solving, reflection and a
tormenting dialectic between artist and work. Yet no matter
what, no matter where and when, art endures and helps one
endure: it has always and everywhere, for the past 30,000 years,
been a source of human expression and invariably a source of
human hope.

In a society where walls dominate everywhere, what better thing to do than learn how to paint a mural? So, at a youth activity centre – Al-Amari Camp – John and Yves helped organize the painting of a mural on the playground wall. With 28 kids and only fourteen paintbrushes there was a lot of borrowing and passing brushes about, and drips and smudged paint everywhere; happy memories, hoped-for dreams, smiling family faces all got softly daubed onto hard stone. One little boy, Berger said, kept recreating the same image over and over again on the wall, and then, the following week, did the same thing in charcoal on paper: a linked line of stick figures, their arms held up high in the air, in a V, all connected by horizontal lines, and always above them he scrawled: 'Al-Aqsa Martyrs Brigade'.

There is no wall in the centre of Ramallah that is not covered with photographs of the dead, taken while they were alive, immortalized as small posters. These are the martyrs of the Second Intifada, which began in late September 2000, after Ariel Sharon visited the Temple Mount, the holiest of sites for Muslims; rioting broke out then and Israeli police eventually gunned down 47 Palestinians. Violence quickly escalated. On the second day of the Intifada Jamal al-Durrah and his twelve-year-old son Muhammad were caught in a crossfire between Israeli soldiers and Palestinian security forces. Father and son cowered behind a concrete cylinder. A freelance Palestinian cameraman, working for France's TV 2, caught the event on camera and later his footage beamed out across the globe.

Lasting just 59 seconds, the images show a crouching pair holding one another, the boy crying as his father shields him from the bullets. Then Jamal waves towards the Israeli soldiers and shouts something. Suddenly there is a burst of gunfire and the camera loses focus amid a swirl of dust, only to return showing Jamal sitting upright, bloody and injured, with his son Muhammad slumped over his legs. The father and son were eventually taken by ambulance to a hospital in Gaza City; but the boy, with multiple gunshot wounds to his arms and abdomen, died en route.

Several days later two Israeli army reservists were lynched in Ramallah by an angry mob of Palestinians reacting to Muhammad al-Durrah's death; the pair were beaten, burned and had their eyes gouged out. The brutality of the killings shocked the Israeli public and immediately the military carried out 'sonic boom' bombings on Ramallah, jet fighter air strikes, low-flying and breaking the sound barrier as they reduced all below to rubble. In March 2002, under 'Operation Defensive Shield', Israeli forces once again occupied the Arab city, heralding more bulldozing and curfews, more school closures and even more intensified control of Palestinian movement.

The enormity of the mismatch in weaponry, Berger says, can be felt on the grief-stricken walls that everywhere bear pictures of the dead. Many are only young boys like Muhammad, boys who left school prematurely, boys born in refugee camps, boys who will never work; these are the same boys who fabricate catapults from carved wood, twined rope and twisted leather, catapults that hurl stones at the occupying army. Slingshots, catapults, worn Kalashnikovs and homemade explosives pit themselves against Apache and Cobra helicopters, F-16s, tanks, Humvee jeeps, tear gas and all manner of high-tech electronic surveillance gadgetry. Nonetheless 'the time of the victors', says Berger in 'A Moment in Ramallah', 'is always short and that of the defeated unaccountably long'. They still have time on their side, because as the living get older, martyrs somehow grow younger, are somehow in a state of perpetual becoming. 'Their space is different, too. Everything in this limited land is a question of space, and the victors have understood as much. The stranglehold they maintain is first and foremost spatial.' It's about total terrestrial domination: The in-ex-or-ab-le hell of geography . . .

On the outskirts of Ramallah is a small hill called Al Rabweh, at the end of Tokyo Street. The street is called 'Tokyo' because along it there's a cultural centre built exclusively through Japanese funding. At the top of this hill – 'the hill with green grass on it' – Palestine's unofficial Poet Laureate, Mahmoud Darwish, is buried. Poet of dispossession and exile, of death and resurrection, Darwish wanted to be put to rest in his native village of Al-Birweh in Galilee, where he was born in 1942 and where his almost-centenarian mother still lives; but the Israeli authorities forbade it. His funeral, in early August 2008, was attended by tens of thousands of people and three days of national mourning were declared. (Palestinian authorities issued four postage stamps commemorating the dead poet.) 'He's the son of you all', Darwish's mother said, addressing the crowd of mourners.

When Berger and son Yves made their pilgrimage to Darwish's Al Rabweh shrine two months after his burial, during another visit to Palestine for an artist's workshop, the hill was deserted. They squatted down, Berger recalls, remembering Darwish's 'calm voice of a beekeeper'. The earth was newly dug and beside the headstone those who had paid their respects had left little sheaves of green wheat, as Darwish requested in his epic work, *Mural*, in which he had imagined his own death and reincarnation.[3] 'Place seven ears of green wheat on my coffin and a few red anemones should you find them / otherwise leave the roses for churches and newly-weds.' Maybe here father and son mourners could also hear Darwish's voice addressing them: 'Take it easy – perhaps you're worn out by star wars / Who am I that you should visit me? / Have you had time to check out my poem? / No that's not your concern / your concern is with the clay of man's being.'

Darwish and Berger had known each other for years, not brilliantly well, not closely, but were at ease with one another, understood one another. In many ways they resembled each other: they were both poets not of winners and conquering heroes but of underdogs, of the vulnerable and the unsung heroes of everyday life, those who more frequently *lose*. But in losing they never lose hope, and Darwish's poetry bought out what was heroic in that everyday hope – its determination as well as its vulnerability. In posing questions about death, so often prevalent in Darwish's verse, 'I make hymns to life', he said.

> The most important lesson I've taken from this is that life is a most beautiful thing, an inestimable gift from God; and we should live out our time intensely. As for an eternal life, we haven't learnt anything more since the days of Gilgamesh. The theme has solicited diverse religious responses; but, as a poet, I don't like those and don't want to mix them up in poetry. People believe in what they know; many more believe in what they don't know. The essential, in struggling between life and death, is to choose life.[4]

Darwish teaches us to mistrust the explicitly political poem, and to privilege what is intimate, what appears the most ordinary because the most ordinary contains its own mythical and metaphysical dimension.

Nowhere is this mythical and metaphysical dimension so evident as in Darwish's *Mural*. When people build high walls we can defy them and defy the death they render by painting them with our own colours, with our own peace paint. During the period coinciding with Darwish's death, Berger was busily at work with the Palestinian anthropology professor Rema Hammami, collaborating on a new translation of *Mural*. (The subject-matter of death cannot have been entirely lost on an octogenarian translator either.) Other translations of *Mural* exist; but 'the question', Berger says in *Le blaireau et le roi*,

> wasn't of knowing if our translation was better or less good than others. The experience of throwing oneself into a translation of

somebody who's alive and then suddenly having to continue it after his death, is a very curious one . . . Darwish amuses himself with his own death. He jokes with it, encircles it, dialogues with it. His disappearance considerably modified our work of translating *Mural*. We knew he would neither have approved nor disapproved of it. But we needed to be absolutely faithful, more faithful than ever: because now his words revealed themselves to us in an even more acute manner.

But 'fidelity' in the act of translation, Berger knows, is never a question of being literal, of finding the exact same words in another language, of claiming some linguistic alikeness to the original. That is the making of a bad translation. Berger knows this from Walter Benjamin, from the latter's essay 'The Task of the Translator', the German critic's introduction to his own translations of Baudelaire. Any translation, Benjamin says, pertinently in the case of Berger's work on Darwish,

issues from the original, not so much from its life as from its afterlife. For a translation comes later than the original, and since the important works of world literature never find their chosen translators at the time of their origin, their translation marks their stage of continued life.[5]

The task of the translator, Benjamin insists, is to capture the 'essential quality' of the original, establish 'a vital connection' with it, renew what is living in it, keep it alive by watching it undergo a 'maturing process'. 'Translation', says Benjamin, 'is so far removed from being the sterile equation of two dead languages that of all literary forms it is the one charged with the special mission of watching over the maturing process of the original language and the birth pangs of its own.' The task of the translator is thus to find the 'intended effect' upon the language, to produce in the translation the echo of the original. Any translation, according to Benjamin, 'must lovingly and in detail incorporate the original's mode of signification'. A good translation is 'transparent': it doesn't block out the light of the original; it allows the pure language to shine upon the original; it does so by a literal translation of *syntax* rather than of actual words. 'For if the sentence is the wall before the language of the original, literalness is the arcade.' We might say, following Benjamin, that Berger and Hammami have painted their own mural onto Darwish's *Mural*: they do so in such a way that readers can see both images simultaneously while only ever being aware of one:

> He into me I into you
> There's neither whole nor parts
> No one living says to the dead: be me!
> . . . elements like feelings dissolve
> But I don't see my body there
> I'm neither the fullness of my death
> nor the fullness of my first life
> As if I'm not made of me
> Who am I?
> The deceased or the newborn?

Berger says he argued incessantly with Rema Hammami during the two years spent translating *Mural*. Berger's style is not con-frontational for the hell of it, but knows that collaboration can never mean compromise: you have to fight for your side, tough it out with your co-worker; all differences of opinion have to be confronted; you have to find an agreed upon solution to a problem, to a word, to a breath. And there is never any concession or conceding in the resolution.

Berger and Hammami's arguments were professional arguments, arguments amongst dear friends, forever dear friends, arguments of collaboration, arguments about what lay *behind* Darwish's original Arabic, how it could find its English afterlife. 'Translation is such a subtle process', Berger says: 'you have to penetrate the language, get behind it. You have to find the rhythm, the silences. What we had was a voice – Darwish's in English, which has its own rhythm, cadence, forms of silence' (interview with *The New Statesman*, 18 January 2010). As it happened, Darwish did live to see the result, did read Berger's 'very free' translation of *Mural*. 'He was surprised by it', Berger says, 'yet later admitted that, yes, somewhere there is my voice.'[6]

Death
wait for me
at the door to the sea in the café of romantics
Don't come back until your arrow misses one last time
Like this I can say farewell to my inside from my outside
Like this I can proffer my wheat-filled soul to blackbirds
    perched on my hand and shoulder
Like this I can say goodbye to the land that drinks my salt
    and sows me as pasture for the horses and gazelles
Wait whilst I finish my short visit to time and place
Don't argue about whether or not I'm coming back
I'm going to thank life
while neither living nor dead
Death the supreme one you're the orphan!
 . . . Green the land of my poem is green and high
Slowly I tell it slowly with the grace of a seagull riding
    the waves on the book of water
I bequeath it written down to the one who asks: to whom
    shall we sing when salt poisons the dew?
 . . . I am the grain that died and became green again
there is something of life in death . . .
I said: am I still here freed or captured without knowing it?

Is the sea behind the walls my sea?
He said: you're a prisoner, prisoner of yourself and
   nostalgia!
The me you see isn't me – I am my ghost
So I say speaking to myself: I am alive
and I ask: If two ghosts meet in the desert do they share
   the sand
or fight for monopoly of the night?[7]

The spirit of a defiant Darwish, of cultural resistance within ordinary everyday life, is not lost in Berger's novel *From A to X*, shortlisted for the 2008 Booker Prize, a novel of 'recuperated letters' written by A'ida to an incarcerated Xavier. The latter has been condemned to life, two life sentences in fact, for acts of resistance that seemingly have 'terrorist' implications. We never hear exactly what Xavier did, but we know he was the mastermind behind a network of subversives. And we know enough, even if we never hear it from Xavier himself, that, as the last prisoner in the old maximum-security prison, in a cell measuring 2.5 by 3 metres, he kept abreast of the news and read a lot: from Fanon to Galeano, and Chavez to Debord, from *F to G*, and from *C to D*. 'All usurpers do their utmost to make us forget that they have only just arrived.'

A'ida and Xavier were never married and so A'ida has no visiting rights; she can never meet her lover again. All she has is the power of words, words to overcome the separation, words to penetrate the walls; sensual letters, letters from the overground to the underground, *Persian Letters* in which pharmacist A'ida reveals all, gives us her heart laid bare. Some letters are so intense that A'ida can't bring herself to send them; others remark upon the ostensibly trivial comings and goings of a lone woman trying to piece together life in the ruins, of how she fills in the absence, displaces her yearning. (We are never told what country we are in, yet the dryness and the dust, the atmosphere of claustrophobic surveillance, of military air raids and clandestine revolt, is somehow Middle Eastern: 'It's very dry; it hasn't rained for two months . . . Gassan wasn't there when his house was destroyed. He had gone to the market and was playing cards with some cronies. When he heard the news, he foundered and fell to the floor, making no sound.') What unfolds in *From A to X* is a tale of undying love in a time of cholera, an epoch when smart people everywhere know that IMF, WB, GATT, WTO, NAFTA, FTAA are acronyms which 'gag language, as their actions stifle the world'. It's just that, as yet, smart people haven't quite figured out what to do about all this . . .

At times the correspondence between A and X smacks of doom and of being as mawkish as that of Abélard and Héloïse; and yet A'ida's letters are too gritty, too determined to suggest passivity. Besides, as the narrator 'J. B.' writes in his prologue,

> A'ida obviously chose not to refer in her letters to her ongoing life as an activist. Occasionally, however, she couldn't resist what I suspect to be a reference. This is how I interpret her remarks about the playing canasta. I doubt whether she played canasta. Following the same prudence, she surely changed the names of close acquaintances, as well as place names . . .

Occasionally, too, A'ida can't hold herself back from letting rip, from venting spleen:

> Across the world, uniformed, highly armed, commanded soldiers operate against captured unarmed civilians, temporarily isolated and surrounded. This is the new military profession . . . Soldiers have been transformed into bastards . . . The old military orders of Advance and Withdraw or Offer Covering Fire have become obsolete because there is no frontline and no opposing army. Nobody will say of one of these bastards that he died nobly . . . (Letter unsent).

Other letters are expressive of a simpler tenderness and vulnerability: 'I'm writing to you. Now I look down at my hands that want to touch you and they seem obsolete because they haven't touched you for so long. Your A'ida.' 'Night has fallen, there's a power cut, I can hear a drone surveying us from the sky, and I put my hands between yours before getting into bed with a candle. Your A'ida.' 'I hurry back to the car, trembling. When I'm in the driver's seat, I put my forehead against the steering wheel and I weep. I weep. I fell asleep weeping. I don't know for how long. A passing lorry woke me . . . (Letter unsent).' 'To be in the world is pain – the poem is true – and my hands tonight want to console you.' 'In the morning, from my pillow, I like to watch you standing there, at the foot of our bed, and you screw up your eyes and you have to undo three buttons before you can slip it over your head. Two thousand, one hundred and twenty-six days. Your eternal A'ida.'

At first blush A'ida seems like another classic fictional Berger character: a strong, independent woman. The lineage is long: from Beatrice and Nusa in *G.*, the Cocadrille and Odile in *Pig Earth* and *Once in Europa*, Zsuzsa and Ninon in *Lilac and Flag* and *To the Wedding*, Daria and Vica in *A Question of Geography* and *King*, to A'ida in *From A to X*, Berger has often chosen to frame his creative universe, to interrogate the nature of the world, from the standpoint of a female.[8] And yet is this really so here? Is A'ida really a strong *woman*? Can we believe in her and in her letters? Does she take us into her world and inside those prison walls? One has doubts. For despite the tender humanity, despite the wonderful eye for evoking everydayness, Berger's A'ida never quite convinces us: we somehow know, know instinctively, that her letters are written by J. B., by a John Berger who has something *political* in mind, who is struggling to give artistic form to his pissed-offness with the world, with its rulers' hypocrisy and injustices.

We might wonder this time whether Berger would have been better off coming clean as a man, surprising us with a heroic male lead. Perhaps those letters should have been written by Xavier, from his standpoint, from inside the four walls, a prisoner's diary, Solzhenitsyn-style, notes from the neoliberal political underground. That way the two lovers could have had a dialogue and readers could have read both sides of their correspondence, got to know their respective characters in the flesh; then, too, the narrative could have flowed back and forth more compellingly, more dramatically, less self-consciously.

We might even wonder whether *From A to X* lent itself to the novelistic genre at all, even to a form so admittedly quirky. Perhaps late-Berger is better adept at non-fiction, at short essays and short stories in which art and real life are embellished poetically, are given fictional twists that reveal new, hidden facts. (Perhaps late-Berger is too angry to mix fiction with politics, given that much politics is itself fictitious. Arundhati Roy comes to mind as somebody who has put her fictional talents aside for the moment, dedicating herself explicitly to political activism and straight-talking polemics. 'When I write something', she said recently, 'I have to spend a few days filtering out the fury.'[9])

One only has to think of the raging, credulous beauty of Berger's *Hold Everything Dear* (2007) (whose title comes from Gareth Evans's poem), a collection of 'Dispatches on Survival and Resistance', in which artistry and activism, poetry and political muckraking, mesh lucidly and movingly, and have no real need to disguise themselves in any art form other than what they are: John Berger's art form, his own special way of telling true stories about what corporate, military and paramilitary muscle does to places and ordinary people. In *Hold Everything Dear* we can grasp, take with us, what we cannot quite take from *From A to X*: *another side of desire*, the sensual desire of the dispossessed, of those seeking to confront walls, dividing walls, of people who want to break on through to the other side. 'The sirens wail down the street', Berger says in 'Another Side of Desire' (cf. *Hold Everything Dear*). 'As long as you are in my arms, no harm will come to you.'

Berger admits how two Fayum portraits of a man and a woman, painted in Egypt nearly 2,000 years ago, inspired him to write *From A to X*.[10] Their faces, reproduced in colour at the beginning and end of *From A to X*, are remarkably fresh looking, remarkably twenty-first century: stoic yet hopeful, still alive and kicking even after all those years of being worn away. The images look a little like brother and sister; but their noses are sufficiently different, and there's a certain twinkle in each other's eyes, a certain manner of *scanning* one another, that suggests they are in fact lovers, models for A'ida and Xavier.

Their vitality is all the more surprising because Fayum portraits were never meant for posterity: they were images destined to accompany the sitter to his or her grave. The artist was Death's painter, a painter of portraits without any future, those to be mummified in an eternal, sepulchral darkness. But Berger exhumes two such portraits, resuscitates them, brings them back to light and life, and places their beeswax gaze before us, so that the once dead can judge the still living. As we close *From A to X*, put its two covers together, the dead lovers enter one another; their passionate embrace lets us accept their parting as a demarcation rather than separation, as a *fold* rather than a wall. Indeed, 'the fold' might actually be the nemesis of our contemporary penchant for walls. Folds, after all, express a Leibniz-like monad, a society in which all reality folds around itself as in origami; all boundaries between the inside and outside, organic and inorganic, nature and culture, animal and human, cease, and instead assume one continuous flowing 'texturology'.[11]

Berger himself has already given us a glimpse of what this folding universe resembles, this utopian ideal where walls, if they exist, only prop up rather than keep out. The 'Ideal Palace', the great peasant work of art by the Facteur Cheval, is one reality in which there are no actual exterior surfaces: every surface, every wall, is a kind of fold, Berger says, something that refers you *inwards*. When life becomes art, and literature materializes as sculpture, as a built form, what we have is not so much a 'machine for living in' as 'a muse for wandering in', a poem that's a never-ending monument, a palace that's not really a palace but a forest. Within it, Berger says,

> are contained many smaller palaces, chateaux, temples, houses, lairs, earths, nests, holes, etc. Each time you enter it, you see something different . . . Whether you climb up its towers, walk through its crypts or look up at a façade from the ground, you are aware of having *entered* something.[12]

What surrounds you is physical reality, made of sandstone and tufa, sand and quicklime, shells and fossils; but it is a sensual, mineral reality, too, a whole living and breathing organic being:

> A kind of tissue connects everything. You can think of it as consisting of leaves, folds, follicles, or cells. All Cheval's sustained energy, all his faith, went into creating this. It is in this tissue that you feel the actual rhythm of his movements as he moulded the cement or placed his stones. It was in seeing this tissue grow beneath his hands that he was confirmed. It is this tissue which surrounds you like a womb.

Each fold, each tissue, is a kind of leaf, yet an archetypal leaf in the sense that Goethe portrays it, a leaf from which all plant forms derive, from which all life spawns. Here walls do not so much confront as nurture: *nurturing* walls, walls dear to Berger's heart, walls of welcome and hospitality, not walls of fear and contempt.

Nurturing Walls is a collection of photographs of murals painted by Meena tribal women in Rajasthan, paintings designed on walls and floors and courtyards of village houses. Here simple shapes come to life as animals, as birds and insects, as vividly decorated fauna and flora painted exclusively in white on exterior brown mud surfaces. The outside becomes part of the interior living room; negative space becomes positive space, and private space becomes public art; all passers-by are beckoned in not shooed away. Domesticity gets redefined; the 'female' sensibility emphasizes connectedness, reproduction and nurture, primal bonds between mother and child, both human and animal.

Nurturing Walls, published in October 2008, is an *artisanal* product, silk-screen printed and stitched together by hand on handmade paper. Berger publicly introduced it and launched an exhibition of Meena art at London's Rebecca Hossack Gallery. 'If one thinks of the global world order', Berger said that evening,

> of its economic fascism, it is increasingly obvious that more and more walls are being built, walls of segregation, walls to keep the poor out, in Palestine and along the Mexican border. These Meena walls are the exact opposite of this: they're walls of welcome; they're *resistant* walls, because they aren't like the walls encroaching around us today. On them are images of animals, animals because animals encircle, animals reproduce, because they have a kind of *alacrity*, a kind of speed. There's speed *within* these pictures. These animals *wink* at you, have a sense of humour; they know things. They let us know that we are all guests and that here tonight we accept their hospitality and we say thank you!

Such nurturing walls – like the walls of the Ideal Palace, like folding and unfolding tissue – surround you, drape around you like luscious velvet curtains, provide seclusion without exclusion;

Leibniz's fold, or the folds draped around Spinoza's four-poster bed, the one in which he slept all his life, his parents' four-poster bed with its heavy curtains. They enveloped a single body that was really universal substance; they allowed Spinoza to think inwardly about connections with the vast, outward cosmos, a cosmos that incorporates us. Folds of demarcation, folds that permit the passage from one state to another, folds that signify a correspondence between affections of the body and ideas of the mind, an inextricable connection without any forced unification. To affirm the world as a series of folds rather than curse it with a battalion of walls is to stress the world as an encounter, as a site for possible rendezvouses, for keeping rendezvouses. And here, as well as there, no passports or ID cards are required; all movement is, as it were, free-folding.

Perhaps Spinoza's drapes, those pleating around his four-poster bed, were actually wounded red, the colour of John Berger's shirt, the one he wore holding little Melina's hand in front of that Wall. Perhaps if we look at the photo again, look really hard, we can recognize that behind *Papi* Berger's hand-held tenderness lies a pent-up frustration, borne across his shoulders and tilting head, a frustration of the radical citizen in the face of a patent injustice, wanting the whole damn thing to blow, wanting to act *now*, wanting to confront '*That Wall*' – as Hikmet had said. Perhaps Berger would have liked nothing better then than to don his helmet and leathers, to mount his motorbike, press its ignition and try to scale that wall as bike-man Cooler King Steve McQueen had tried to scale those fences in *The Great Escape*. Perhaps we can imagine Berger on his bike, revving it up, accelerating, launching his own great escape from oppression, trying to scale those prison walls and barbed-wire fences that separate us, soaring over them on his flying Blackbird, doing it for little Melina's generation, riding high, onwards, towards eternity . . .

Spinoza's Motorbike

'I shall consider human actions and appetites just as if it were a question
of lines, planes, and bodies.'
Baruch Spinoza, *Ethics*

'That's all the motorcycle is, a system of concepts worked out in steel.
There's no part of it, no shape in it, that is not out of someone's mind.'
Robert Pirsig, *Zen and the Art of Motorcycle Maintenance*

That motorbike, that dulcet-toned Blackbird glimpsed outside
Berger's Quincy farmhouse, isn't only a machine to confront walls;
it is the ticket to ride towards a modern destination, a metaphor of
modern politics, even of modern life. The motorbike is important
to Berger, existentially, politically and artistically. It seems to suggest
something about the quantum gravity of his personality, about the
particle who likes to stay put, in place, and the complementarity of
the flowing radical who restlessly trawls the globe, who functions
in deterritorialized, wavy motorbike space, an uneasy rider on
the road.

Aboard Berger's bike, maybe it's possible to write our own
Zen and the Art of Motorcycle Maintenance, update and upgrade
it for our global age, for our post-Seattle world order, reuniting
technology and poetry, analytical rationality with romance, feeling
the breeze in our hair as we cruise, yet have direction and purpose
to our forward motion. We can hold on to Berger for dear life,

trust him to take us somewhere, over the rainbow, over the mountaintop, over the wall. And because our motorbike is a vehicle – not a juggernaut – he will know how to repair it should it break down, should it grind to a halt in some lay-by. On this journey, on this journey towards a destination, towards a real sense of place – a meeting place – we arrive by accident, by a special means of traveling.

For an ontological road map, we might begin with Berger's essay 'How Fast Does It Go?' from *Keeping a Rendezvous*. Aboard a motorbike, he says, 'except for the protective gear you're wearing, there's nothing between you and the rest of the world. The air and the wind press directly on you. You are *in* the space through which you are traveling.' Your contact with the outside world is more *intimate*. You are more conscious of the road surface, of its subtle variations, its potholes, whether it is dry or damp, made of mud or gravel; you are aware of the hold of the tyres, or their lack of hold; bends produce another effect: 'If you enter one properly, it holds you in its arms. A hill points you to the sky. A descent lets you dive into it. Every contour line on the map of the country you're driving through means your axis of balance has changed . . . This perception is visual but also tactile and rhythmic. Often your body knows quicker than your mind.' Liberty here comes from the relationship between oneself and space, between subjectivity and spatiality, not exclusively from the speed at which you are travelling.

After a few hours of driving across the countryside, you feel you have left behind more than the towns and villages you've been through. You've left behind certain familiar constraints. You feel less terrestrial than when you set out. Supposing at this moment you stop, cut the engine, take off your helmet, stretch your back and your neck, and then walk a few paces along the road, into a wood or a field. You look around. There's nothing spectacular or picturesque. But you've stopped, and this already makes the spot special . . . The point of arrival is unique, and recognizable as such.

Still, the question of speed does not entirely disappear. 'Speed is of the essence', Berger admits. Perhaps this partly explains the Berger paradox: one can imagine him painstakingly drawing in deep quietness, or shaping and reshaping a single sentence of a short story, crafting it until it sounds right, until it has the appropriate musicality, the right tempo, the correct imagery; he will do it for hours and hours on end, patiently, until he has the phrase he wants. At other times it is perhaps easy to imagine Berger eager to get on with things, to get things done, to hasten them along without dilly-dallying; here we can perhaps imagine Berger's impatient streak, his headstrongness, needing to go full throttle, come what may. But by speed he clarifies:

I don't necessarily mean the speed at which you're traveling. The reading on the speedometer is a small part of the story. Time and again people ask, 'How fast does it go?' It's a natural question, for bikes do go fast and they can accelerate quickly. But their relation to the phenomenon and sensation of speed is more complex than a simple reckoning of their top speed.

On a bike the fastness that counts most, like the fastness in life, is, he says,

that between decision and consequence, between action, which is often a reflex action, and effect . . . Other vehicles may in fact react as quickly or more quickly than a motorbike, but a jet plane, a highly tuned car, a speedboat are not as physically close to your body, and none of them leave your body so exposed. From this comes the sensation that the bike is responding as

immediately as one of your own limbs . . . This immediacy
bestows a sense of freedom.

The pilot of a motorbike is constantly leaning their body against
and into the road, counteracting centrifugal force, grappling with
inertia, bending, turning, looping, zigzagging corners, continually
adapting their gaze so as to observe the maximum possible. It's
a *pas de deux*, Berger says, pilot and road locked together in a
passionate embrace, tap-dancing partners along the inexorable
man-machine highway of life.

Some roads are familiar, everyday; others unfamiliar. There
are busy main roads and quiet backwaters (though the latter are
increasingly more difficult to discover). On a motorbike familiar
roads are like members of the family, and one should never take
them for granted. 'Roads', Berger says in his essay 'The Road',

> are a strange mixture between the man-made and the natural.
> Old roads are often brothers or sisters to rivers; they run side
> by side. Certain roads are like teachers to large forests; they
> introduce measure which otherwise doesn't exist in uncrossed
> forests. There are roads who are the children of mountain
> passes. Only autoroutes fail to have this natural side, which
> explains the ferocious solitude they evoke.

Autoroutes are designed on drawing boards by planners and
specialists, intended for indifferent speed; 'on them speed becomes
a flight from loneliness. An anguished impatience to arrive and to
re-find company!'

Berger's essay 'The Road' actually appeared in a very *un*intellectual publication: *Motorcycle International* (February 1993), a fanzine
for biking enthusiasts, for Anglo-American bike lovers. ('As soon
as you are in love', Berger writes, 'there is of course the danger of
being betrayed. Should this happen, the pilot is always the loser.

A miscalculation, a false movement, a lack of imagination, and he hits the hard ground. Not the beloved road but the hard ground.') Accompanying Berger's essay is a well-turned portrait called 'Renaissance Man on a Rocketship', as well as a glossy colour-photo spread of its subject, the leather-clad, helmeted avenger (including one of him making a natural pit stop!). The profile talks about the writer's own early love affair with the road and with motorbikes, such as the BSA Jawa 250 he owned in the 1950s, a machine he thought every socialist should ride; then it was an BSA 500, which he once rode from London to Amsterdam, and onwards to Rome; a few years later Berger set off to Moscow *en moto*, yet in Warsaw the local branch of the KGB denied him entry; not because of politics, but because a motorbike supposedly posed a 'security risk'!

By the time he had got together with Anya Bostock, and kids Jacob and Katya arrived in the early 1960s, for the family man Berger a motorbike became an impractical mode of transport. Two wheels gave way to four, and a succession of 2CVs followed, *Deux Chevaux*, the classic French country machine; take off its bonnet and you can carry anything inside, from goats to firewood, from bootleg *gnôle* to crates of *grand cru*. And so it was after a longish hiatus that Berger later joined the ever-swelling ranks of 'Born Again Bikers', retaking his driving permit in France at the tender age of 62. Since then he has treated himself to a series of bigger bikes, an ascending order of bike-spotter acronyms and numbers: CBR600, VF750, VF1000, CBR1000, and current CBR1100XX (Blackbird). 'John is constantly aware of the vulnerability of bike riding', the article says, 'but in a way it is one of the reasons that he enjoys it so much. That vulnerability makes one very much alive and aware of the surroundings. There's a kind of multi-layered consciousness involved in riding that is very special.'

You have to wonder if Berger ever read *Zen and the Art of Motor - cycle Maintenance*, a two-wheeled cult equivalent to Kerouac's four-wheeled *On the Road*. A lot of what he has to say about motorbikes chimes with Robert Pirsig's profound book from 1974. 'Tensions disappear along old roads like this', Pirsig says, voyaging from Minneapolis to the Dakotas, and over the Rockies to Santa Rosa and San Francisco with his young son Chris in tow, hugging him as Ninon would hug papa Jean in *To the Wedding*. 'We bump along the beat-up concrete between the cattails and stretches of meadow and then more cattails and marsh grass . . . I whack Chris's knee and point up. "What!" he hollers. "Blackbird!"' You see things on a motorcycle, says Pirsig, in a way that's completely different from a car.

> In a car you're always in a compartment, and because you're used to it you don't realize that through that car window everything you see is just more TV.
>
> You're a passive observer and it is all moving by you boringly in a frame. On a cycle the frame is gone. You're completely in contact with it all. You're *in* the scene, not just watching it any - more, and the sense of presence is overwhelming. That concrete whizzing by five inches below your foot is the real thing, the same stuff you walk on, it's right there, so blurred you can't focus on it, yet you can put your foot down and touch it anytime, and the whole thing, the whole experience, is never removed from immediate consciousness.[1]

In *Zen and the Art of Motorcycle Maintenance* Pirsig stresses that on a motorbike you often go more to travel than to arrive. It is the *going* that counts. That *is* the destination; or, if you arrive somewhere, it's frequently *par hasard*, an unintended roadstop, a gem en route, a chance encounter in which disparate roads, a series of random turns, all somehow intersect, all lead you to the *hereness* and *nowness* of a place. 'Secondary roads are preferred', he says.

On the road in the mountains.

Paved country roads are the best, state highways are next. Freeways are the worst. We want to make good time, but for us now this is measured with emphasis on 'good' rather than 'time' and when you make that shift in emphasis the whole approach changes . . . Roads free of drive-ins and billboards are better, roads where groves and meadows and orchards and lawns come almost to the shoulder, where kids wave at you when you ride by, where people look from their porches to see who it is . . . these roads are truly different from the main ones. The whole pace of life along them is different. People aren't too busy to be courteous. The hereness and nowness of things is something they all know about . . .

In a curious way Pirsig's *Zen and the Art of Motorcycle Maintenance* and Berger's *G.* have plenty in common. Both texts are somehow working through the same problematic; and it is no coincidence that they appeared within two years of one another, written by men of the same generation (Berger born 1926, Pirsig 1928), writers with similar passions, similar impulses, who have used motorcycles figuratively to understand the world. Each book, too, could only have been written in the decade of the 1970s, in the post-1960s period, at a time of taking stock, of reconsideration.[2] To a large extent this post-'68 period was also a time of disillusionment, of emptiness, of a breach, and these two books sought to address that breach, tried to leap across it, to build a bridge in between. The dust had settled from countercultural exuberance; people had gone home after the parties, after the be-ins, after the street protests. The 1960s had been the epoch of the orgasm, the groovy dimension of impulse and individual liberty, like G. fucking to his heart's content without structure, without constraint, with neither history nor society getting in his way. Yet in the 1970s reality bit back, turned square: freedom gave way to necessity, the self to society, the individual to repressive institutional order. And after 1973 the economy was upending, going into slump.

The rift between the 1960s and '70s is legion in *G.*, as it is in *Zen and the Art of Motorcycle Maintenance*; Berger aboard his Honda Blackbird and Pirsig aboard his Honda Super Hawk (305 cc), riding along different roads, an ocean apart, take to their motorbikes as well as to their pens to probe it: the *romantic*, intuitive paradigm of an easy rider, of experiencing your bike as poetry, as sensual stimulation, as cruising – epitomized by the heady 1960s – pitted against the *scientific*, factual side of things, the mechanics of the motorcycle, the rational, underlying principles of its maintenance, of checking oil, of technical troubleshooting, responsive to classical Newtonian method – epitomized by the more sober 1970s. By then, the motorbike had broken down and needed fixing. What could poetry do, even art? Something had given way, but what? The individual, apparently, was beholden to some underlying social morality, to the rules of social reality, to the rational order. This

Pit stop in Haute-Savoie.

was G.'s undoing: the crowd that his father detested so much finally got to his wayward son.

At the beginning of the new millennium the dualism persists, exaggerated perhaps because now the worm has turned, now the romantic, intuitive side of riding the motorcycle has been utterly suppressed by 'reason', by a supposed technological fix, by the maintenance of human problems through 'rational' free-market globalization and neoliberalization. It is everywhere, this credo, perceived as normal and eternal: There Is No Alternative (TINA). It is a juggernaut we are riding on now, not a motorbike; or, rather, we are being pushed along by this juggernaut, unable to harness it; it is something that again sets us in a frame, mediates our con - sciousness, takes away our sense of place and space; it is out of control in the name of sound science, of what's best for 'us'. 'There is no horizon there', says Berger in *The Shape of a Pocket*. 'There is no continuity between actions, there are no pauses, no paths, no patterns, no past and no future. There is only the clamour of the disparate, fragmentary present': there's neither Zen nor motorcycle maintenance. The search for wholeness and meaningful experience is, then, a necessary yet elusive task. How to piece together the world picture with a self at the centre, intact and connected? How to unite Being in place with a Becoming over space?

Aboard his Blackbird, Berger gives us a rapprochement of a system of *general concepts* worked out in steel and mechanics with a *specific experience* of intimate connection with the environment, a presentness and hereness as well as a thereness, a sense of going somewhere and elsewhere, a sense of going to a destination. The flight of the Blackbird is thus Berger's journey in search of a sense of place, his quest for a territory of experience. And for Berger the writer, as for Berger the rider, there is a necessity to become a single creature, like Jean Ferrero from *To the Wedding*, knowing 'the gap between command and action is no more than that of a synapse'. At night-time, Jean, says John, is burrowing through the darkness like a mole through the earth, the beam of his light boring the tunnel and the tunnel twisting as the road turns to avoid boulders and to climb. Each corner, as man and machine enter it, receives them and hoicks them up. They come in slow and they leave fast. As they come in, they lie over as much as they can, they wait for the corner to give them its camber, and then they leap away.

The anti-hero of *Zen and the Art of Motorcycle Maintenance* is a Pirsig alter ego character, 'Phaedrus', Plato's famous mouthpiece in a dialogue that employs rhetoric to persuade, a dialogue that adopts the allegory of the charioteer and his horses as the image of love. The horses are vicious and unruly by nature, Plato says, and this 'unruly behaviour impairs its vision of reality'. Thus the horses need to be harnessed, controlled by the disciplined charioteer who, through struggle and toil, manages to restrain the wild beasts. The charioteer, accordingly, is 'the pilot of the soul', the voice of reason, the sobering sense of the mind controlling the frenzied passions of the body; rational self-control replaces the madness of headstrong love. Love requires self-mastery, through which the soul recaptures its vision of an ideal world. 'Take this to heart then, my lad', says Plato in *Phaedrus*, 'and learn the lesson that there is no kindness in the friendship of a lover; its object is the satisfaction of an appetite, like the appetite for food. "As wolves for lambs . . .".'

Reality, for Plato, finds its essential feature in a world of unchanging Forms; the shifting phenomena of the sensible world, the experiential realm of the senses, are but mere copies and im - perfections of the mind. Immortal truths, Plato says, are rational ideas, which are essentially changeless. Here Plato separates out 'horseness' from 'horse', because for him horseness is the only reality, the true and unmoving pure Idea, whereas horse is an unimportant, transitory phenomenon, mere appearance, like motorcycle riding. For Pirsig, as for Phaedrus, the motorbike is 'a system of concepts worked out in steel'. There is no part, no shape of it, that is not fashioned out of somebody's mind, he says. 'That's really what Phaedrus was talking about', Pirsig admits, 'when he said it's all in the mind.' Both Phaedrus and Plato – and the latter is the former's master – believe, as Pirsig believes, that the steel casing of the motorbike is a mere shadow, something necessarily inferior to the idea of an engine, to a mechanical concept generated perfectly within the mind.

Yet for the rider Jean, just as for his alter ego writer John, another ontology, one more *unified* and *materialist*, more *Spinozist* in orientation, replaces this *idealist dualism* of Plato's vision of truth. Spinoza gives all power to the mind *and* body: the Spinozan body is a body that thinks just as the Spinozan mind is a mind that feels. In piloting a motorbike, charioteer and horsepower become one and the same creature, thinking and feeling as human and mechanical beast journey across the slippery plane of immanence.

In *Ethics* Spinoza gives us a remarkable conception of the body, of what bodies have in common, of how bodies can liberate themselves, of how a body frees itself by developing the activity of its *conatus*, its striving and desiring, a feature so apparent in Berger the man and artist. 'The mind and body', Spinoza says, 'are one and the same thing', with the former conceived under the attribute of thought, the latter under the attribute of extension. Bodies *affect* other bodies, and are *affected* by other bodies: it is this capacity for affecting and being affected that defines a body in both its individuality and potential commonality.

For Spinoza, the human mind only knows the human body 'through ideas of affections by which the body is affected'. There is a correspondence between the affections of the body and ideas of the mind, an inextricable connection without any strict causality, a parallelism. For adequate ideas to develop, for our bodies to connect with other bodies, the mind must somehow become conscious of itself *through ideas of the body's affections*. At that point, sad bodies strive to become joyful bodies. Labouring and consuming bodies, bodies that work and bodies that eat, bodies that dig the land and bodies that tap keyboards, exploited bodies and downtrodden bodies, dispossessed bodies, all find unity, all embrace one another; together they 'strive to imagine those things that increase or aid the body's power of acting'.

For years, almost forever, Spinoza has fascinated the biker Berger. In Spinoza Berger has searched for and subsequently found something, something more timeless and joyous, something more inventive and positive; perhaps, too, more recently, Berger believes that with Spinoza he can define a new *affective* politics. Spinoza lets Berger move *within* Marxism, move within its 'critique of capitalist political-economy', within neoliberal flows of capital and trade. Spinoza's materialism is not defined by a 'logic of capital' but is a materialism defined by the subject, a materialism of subjectivity, of the body, one that gives a new language to help Berger think about rebellion, to name it *inside* global capitalism, *inside* ourselves. In this sense it is a mode of thinking that is at once more metaphysical and more concrete, more in tune with Berger's own personality. With it, perhaps Berger can fill in a gap in Marx, a lack; perhaps he can also clarify Marx, because here, with Spinoza, he can affirm peoples' *spirit* in their struggle for liberation. Indeed, when we strive as human beings, Spinoza says, we possess powers as yet unknown even to us.

Berger's most recent book, *Bento's Sketchbook* (2011), is devoted to Spinoza; not so much to a lens-polisher-philosopher Spinoza as to a Spinoza – 'Bento', as he was sometimes known – who carried for most of his life a small sketchbook. Anyone who knew the with - drawn philosopher knew that when he wasn't polishing lenses or developing philosophical propositions he drew images in this sketchbook, likely amateurish images. But after his death in 1677 (at the age of 44), nobody knew of the sketchbook's whereabouts. For years Berger has imagined Bento's sketchbook being found, miraculously turning up, 'not knowing what he hoped to find in it', he says, 'but wanting to reread his words while being able to look at the things Bento had seen with his own eyes'. Berger wants to contemplate the reality Spinoza saw, somehow illustrate himself Bento's thoughts.[3]

Berger also wants to take Spinoza for a spin on his Blackbird: 'Coming for a ride, Bento?' 'I wouldn't make a direct comparison between a motorbike and a telescope for which you ground lenses', he writes in *Bento's Sketchbook*, addressing the dead philosopher,

> yet they have certain features in common: both need to be well-aimed, both diminish distance, and both offer a tunnel of attention and the sensation of speed . . . In the tunnel of speed there is also a kind of silence, and when you get off the bike or remove your eye from the eyepiece, all the slow repetitive sounds of daily life return, and the silence recedes.

But, again, that notion of speed is only a fastness between decision and consequence, between action and effect; Berger's Blackbird key ring, adorned with its little black tortoise, hints of how he has heeded the warning of the tortoise and the hare parable; of how he, too, understands what Pirsig means by making '*good* time'.

As with a telescope, you pilot a motorbike with your eyes. All things always come back to *ways of seeing* for Berger, his eternal recurrence. Ways of riding are, then, really only ways of seeing, and ways of drawing, too. 'For many years I've been fascinated by a certain parallel between the act of piloting a bike and the act of drawing. The parallel fascinates me because it may reveal a secret. About what? About displacement and vision. Looking brings closer.'

Think of a motorbike's trajectory as something similar to a line drawn of the ground. The pilot with his body concentrates hard on maintaining that line; when a drawer makes contact with paper, like a rider with this ground, you immediately assess how absorbent that paper is, how smooth it is, how resistant, how accommodating or intractable, and then you apply the pressure of the pen or the force of the throttle; you steer and you turn, you weave and slow down, you speed up and react as you move across the paper-ground. 'You are riding a drawing', Berger says; you traverse an immanent plane, cross over contours, journey across *smooth* space, folding, unfolding and refolding as you go, an old nomadic biker of newer insane times.

In *Bento's Sketchbook* Spinoza is the star of the show, even if in person his role is only a cameo, passing judgement here and there, with little nuggets from *Ethics* and *Treatise on the Correction of the Intellect*, which dart out in front of you as you turn the *Sketchbook*'s pages. 'The human body needs for its preservation many other bodies from which it is, so to speak, continually regenerated.' 'The mind, in so far as it has both clear and distinct and confused ideas, endeavours to persist in its being for an indefinite period, and is conscious of this its endeavour.' 'A man is affected with the same emotion of pleasure or pain from the image of a thing past or future as from the image of a thing present.'

Spinoza is there in *Bento's Sketchbook*, there between the lines, covert, covert like a private investigator, like *Columbo*'s Peter Falk playing himself in Wim Wenders's *Wings of Desire*, there keeping tabs, there keeping mind and body together, body and soul whole; there so image and desire get closer and closer to one another, there so the self of what is being drawn can enter the self of the drawer. Berger's mind strives to imagine, strives to draw, only those things that increase his power of acting: 'all spontaneous (as distinct from ordered) drawings', he says, '"take off" and are upheld by a similar imaginative movement'. All spontaneous uprisings 'take hold' and are upheld by a similar imaginative movement, fusing people together, letting them emulsify like mayonnaise, freeze like water, curdle like milk, take off as one substance.

'The more an image is joined with many other things', Berger cites Spinoza, 'the more often it flourishes. The more an image is joined with many other things, the more causes there are by which it can be excited.' Images abound in *Bento's Sketchbook*, drawn by the author himself; and pensive commentaries that touch and move you, that sometimes make you laugh, that often leave you wondering, accompany these images. Each drawing is an encounter with a person and a thing: with plums and irises, with dead peasants and sleeping cats, with Spanish dancers and surly security guards (at London's National Gallery, leading to Berger's expulsion), with *The Brothers Karamazov* and Cambodian swimmers in a suburban Parisian pool. Each image, each proposition, suggests rather than tells; invariably it is up to us to figure out what is being suggested, what is hidden between the lines, how the image connects with the words. 'There are two categories of storytelling', Berger says.

> Those that treat of the invisible and the hidden, and those that expose and offer the revealed. What I call – in my own special and physical sense of the terms – the introverted category and the extroverted one. Which of the two is likely to be more adapted to, more trenchant about, what is happening in the world today? I believe the first.

Drawings and politics alike take off because of 'common notions'. They take off because bodies and minds *share* something, because they empathize around similar intuitive reason, because they replace *passive* affects with *active* ones. The hidden is not so much revealed as it becomes a common clandestinity; the invisible a common invisibility. This seems to be what Berger is trying to transmit, trying to let us glimpse, share, in *Bento's Sketchbook*: common notions. Meanwhile, as we near the end, if there can ever be any end to a project like Berger's, somehow we sense, somehow we *feel*, that this book represents a species of eternity, that this is the purity of Berger's art, its greatest virtue to date, beyond duration, beyond space: there's a lightness of touch that strangely resembles the disarming 'geometrical' deftness of Spinoza's own *Ethics*. We might even say that it's the culmination of all those years on the job, the 60-odd years of restless activity, of writing and thinking, of drawing and riding, of meeting and discussing, the finally achieved 'blessedness' and sense of mortality of Spinoza's 'third kind of knowledge', a knowledge that Berger has spent a lifetime searching for, trying to acquire. 'I live in a state of habitual confusion', says Berger. 'By confronting the confusion I sometimes achieve a certain lucidity. You showed us how to do this.'

When we, as individuals, become cognizant of 'common notions', Spinoza says, we develop 'adequate ideas' about ourselves, begin to reason a 'second kind of knowledge.' We begin, in other words, to piece together certain formulations about our lives, certain *relationships* we have with people: we universalize, make more coherent what seems, on the face of it, only specific experience, often vague, confused – 'inadequate' – everyday experience, all of which operates at a 'first kind of knowledge'. And yet what appears to us as particular is really general; what seems just our plight is actually the plight of many people, the plight of a multi-tude of different people, and we identify with this, make links, establish relations, tune in.

To shift between first and second kinds of knowledge is, for Spinoza, precisely an *encounter*, an encounter of humans rendez - vousing with themselves and with one another; not always directly, but intuitively, deductively, through a mode of relating to the world, through unwritten and unstated common agreement, through solidarity, through shared imagery. But that's not all; that can never be all, for either Spinoza or Berger. To be sure, as soon as people begin to find one another, touch one another ideationally, emotionally and experientially, as soon as *we* begin to reach into ourselves as human beings, as beings beyond any specific space and time – as soon as we begin to discover ourselves as 'eternal' beings – only then do we begin to affirm a 'third' kind of knowledge; only then does a singular substance become the common essence of us all; only then does the object of our knowledge and the real object find agreement. The drawer and the drawing, the rider and the machine, become one.

This movement to a third kind of knowledge expresses the *religiosity* Berger has discreetly affirmed over the years, a religiosity that has, as a 'believer', increasingly seeped into the ontological fabric of his work and Being. Needless to say this is not a religiosity of institutions, of churches and commissars, of higher powers; it's not a God who's above us, a God who's a transcendent creator and who offers us freedom *after* death, in heaven. For Berger there's no 'will of God', because the will of God, he knows, after Spinoza, 'is the sanctuary of ignorance'. Berger's God is monadal and metaphysical, like Spinoza's, a single substance with infinite attributes, inside us, outside us in nature, inside both us *and* nature, an immanent essence that we can tap without mediation or mediators, something we can live with, experiment with, write about and of course sketch out.

And so, too, is the Godhead in the Blackbird, in the Blackbird we can now hear starting up, revving up one last time, ready for its journey back home, back to its foyer. So long, we might say, like the Woody Guthrie song, it's been GOOD TO KNOW YOU! I hope we know you a little better now, and hope to see and hear that Blackbird of yours rumbling on, staying on the road for a while longer yet, sailing over those walls, flying high over those lakes like Marcos's heron. So long! Let's fly together, beside Jean Ferrero, beside Jean Berger, beside Bento Berger. We are only waiting for this moment to arrive. Fly Blackbird, fly . . . fly into the light of the dark black night . . .

References

Introduction: The Blackbird, the Badger and the King

1 For the record, Berger once told me he could never remember such a
   dinner ever taking place: he's sure his late friend Cartier-Bresson (who
   died in 2004 aged 95) never came to Quincy. He and Cartier-Bresson
   periodically dined together in Paris, and Dyer must have been present
   on one occasion. At Quincy Berger has local friends who are plumbers
   and they certainly do sometimes dine at his place. Dyer must have been
   there for one soirée and perhaps, Berger thinks, conflated two separate
   meetings into a single, mythical meal. But Dyer's main point, of course,
   still stands: Berger isn't only a democratic writer; he's equally a pro-
   foundly democratic person.
2 Berger, 'A Load of Shit', *Keeping a Rendezvous* (London, 1992), pp. 38–9.
3 Berger's essay 'A Story of Aesop', framed around Velázquez's 1640 image,
   comes from *Keeping a Rendezvous*. In the same book, several pages earlier,
   there's a pencil drawing that Berger made of his mother 'as a stoic';
   her head bears an uncanny resemblance to that of Velázquez's Aesop,
   a likeness surely not lost on Berger himself, who seems to want to weep
   on each of their shoulders.
4 'The Secretary of Death' appears in Berger's collection *The White Bird*
   (London, 1988).
5 *To the Wedding* became both prescient and personally painful for
   Berger: during its writing his own daughter-in-law, the Spanish wife
   of son Jacob, was diagnosed as seropositive and would later develop
   AIDS. Berger says he had already begun *To the Wedding* before any of
   this became known. The novel, then, wasn't motivated by a familial
   tragedy but rather by a global tragedy, though later the text would be

haunted and inspired by something dreadfully close to home. Berger still gives the royalties from *To the Wedding* to London Lighthouse, an organization which supports people living with AIDS. Shortly after the novel's publication, Berger's daughter-in-law died from her illness (Berger, conversation with the author, 9 February 2011).

6 Berger, *Le blaireau et le roi* [*The Badger and the King*] (Geneva, 2010), p. 20.

1 Seeing Eye

1 Geoff Dyer, 'Marxist Scourge Seeking Redemption in the Ashes', *The Guardian*, 30 January 1992.

2 Berger, 'The Production of the World', *The White Bird* (London, 1988), p. 280.

3 Edward Said, *Representations of the Intellectual* (New York, 1993), p. 55.

4 Berger, conversation with the author, 28 June 2011.

5 See *Hold Everything Dear: Dispatches on Survival and Resistance* (London, 2007), p. 32.

6 Berger's Moore diatribe was republished in *Permanent Red* (London, 1960). This citation appears on p. 84.

7 Lavin's character was so convincingly real that Berger once received a letter from a Hungarian woman who worked at the University of Budapest, asking where she might find Lavin's paintings.

8 Stephen Spender, 'Mixing Paint with Politics', *The Observer*, 9 November 1958.

9 Berger, 'Afterword, 1988', *A Painter of Our Time* (London, 1998), p. 198.

10 The question was posed in French in 2007 at a reading Berger did at a suburban Paris bookstore, Librairie le livre écarlate, in Champigny-sur-Marne (see www.livingscoop.com, accessed 13 July 2011).

11 Berger's essay 'Caravaggio: A Contemporary View' is downloadable at www.studio-international.co.uk, accessed 13 July 2011.

12 Dibb, however, sees 'Ways of Seeing' a bit differently. The programme, he once told me, was a product of the 'devolved freedom' then available at the BBC; that it was low-budget meant it could be trusted, meant it was somehow done in a 'protected space'. The programme was actually commissioned by the BBC, by Sir John Drummond, the Executive Producer, and it was believed in. 'Ways of Seeing' did get

full institutional support and backing, Dibb says, and when it won a BAFTA in 1972 for 'Best Specialized Series', sincerest congratulations came from the BBC's higher echelons.

13 Berger, 'Look at it this Way for a Change', *The Guardian*, 29 July 1994.

2 *G.* and Un-*G.*

1 In his 1986 monograph, *Ways of Telling: The Work of John Berger* (London, 1986), Geoff Dyer reckons '*The Foot of Clive* is a bad novel that should have been a play' (p. 45); *Corker's Freedom*, meanwhile, 'is the only one of Berger's books with any light-hearted intention but the oddly stilted diction and the characteristic deliberateness of his prose work against humour' (p. 53).

2 Anya Bostock translated Lukács' text into English (from German) (see *The Theory of the Novel*, London, 1978). Berger told me he was privy to Bostock's work on Lukács and read all the translation in progress. His poem 'At Remaurian' (1962/3), written about a hamlet near Nice, not so far from Bonnieux in the Vaucluse, has Man Ray-esque photos of a naked Anya haunting the Alpes-Maritimes scrubland (see *Pages of the Wound: Poems, Drawings, Photographs, 1956–96*, London, 1996).

3 Lukács quotes Novalis's phrase in his opening chapter; Berger cites it in an unusual book, even by his own unusual standards: *And Our Faces, My Heart, Brief as Photos* (London, 1984), an assortment of stories, poems, and polemics. 'Never before our time have so many people been uprooted', Berger says (pp. 54–5), framing Novalis. 'Emigration, forced or chosen, across national frontiers or from village to metropolis, is the quintessential experience of our time . . . All the modern historians from Marx to Spengler have identified the contemporary phenomenon of emigration. Why add more words? To whisper for that which has been lost. Not out of nostalgia, but because it is on the site of loss that hopes are born.'

4 Berger, *G.* (London, 1989), p. 111.

5 Ibid., p. 112.

6 Jean-Paul Sartre, *Critique of Dialectical Reason – Volume One* (London, 1976), p. 524.

7 'The Nature of Mass Demonstrations' is reprinted in the best collection

of Berger's scattered and diverse articles and commentaries, *John Berger: Selected Essays*, ed. Geoff Dyer (New York, 2001), pp. 246–9.

8 When Berger went *en famille* to Palestine in 2008, in a theatre in Ramallah, under a curfew and with the menacing presence of the Israeli military, he read aloud passages on crowds from *G*. Amid charged and frayed emotions, he read to a crowd of Palestinian men, women and children who identified themselves as kindred with the participants of 1898. 'I had the impression', Berger said, 'of having written the chapter for this precise moment in Ramallah, more than thirty years later.'

3 Van Gogh's Boots

1 Berger, *Pig Earth* (London, 1979), p. 6.

2 The same can't quite be said about the Bergers' son Yves, born (1976) and raised in the village, a native Savoyard and aspiring painter, a bilingual product of experience-near and experience-far, a global citizen and *gars* from the 'hood. While it's true that Yves can leave any time, too, his choice about staying or going isn't the same as his parents'. Quincy *is* the centre of his universe, his monad that internalizes the whole world. The mountains are *his* mountains, not something he's adopted. Interestingly, father and son dialogue (in French, convened by Emmanuel Favre) around issues of belonging, and of art and politics, of what's interior and exterior, is in an underrated little book, *Le blaireau et le roi*. The text warrants an English translation.

3 Berger, *Pig Earth*, p. 11.

4 Ibid., 'Historical Afterword', pp. 211–12.

5 Ibid., pp. 212–13.

6 Little surprise, perhaps, that there are very few peasant artists who have expressed directly the peasant condition. True, plenty of peasant masons, artisans and sculptors have worked on cathedrals, churches and holy sites; but there they expressed the ideology of the Church rather than real peasant experience. One colossal work, 'Le Palais Idéal', is, however, an extraordinary exception to the rule. Thirty-three years in the making, this 'palace passing all imagination', single-handedly built by Ferdinand Cheval (1836–1924), a peasant-postman from the Drôme

département, crumbles yet still stands today in Hauterives, its creator's native village. The palace, says Berger in 'The Ideal Palace' (see *Keeping a Rendezvous*, London, 1992), is determined by two qualities: its *physicality* in stone, sandstone, fossils and shells, and its discrete *innerness*, emphasizing what lies within, the very opposite of the urban experience which concentrates on what is outside. Mysterious architectural forms, figurative sculptures of animals, plants and birds, texts and poetry literally hacked into sheer rock, all represent 'a living organic system'. The Surrealist André Breton made a pilgrimage to the palace in the 1930s; ditto Situationist Guy Debord in the 1950s: both hailed it as a physical realization of fantasy, as a space 'where dreams become reality'. Berger says it's wrong to see the palace as dream-like; it's a mistake to psychologize it: the palace, he thinks, represents what it really is: the enormous, visceral, physical labour of its construction.

7 'It was her last year at school', Berger's tale goes (*Pig Earth*, p. 107), 'that Lucie was given the nickname of the Cocadrille. A *cocadrille* comes from a cock's egg hatched in a dung heap. As soon as it comes out of its egg, it makes its way to the most unlikely place.' When *Pig Earth* was translated into French, its literal equivalent – *Sale Terre, Cochonne de Terre* – meant very little in that language. So *Pig Earth* bore the label *La Cocadrille*, and henceforth the Cocadrille became synonymous with the universal peasant.

8 The Cocadrille's story, 'The Three Lives of Lucie Cabrol', has been put on stage, too, adapted by Simon McBurney's Théâtre de Complicité. The play premiered at the Manchester Dancehouse in January 1994, and later toured Britain, including London's West End, before sell-out audiences. In McBurney's 'exhilarating production', *The Guardian* wrote, 'the story becomes an unsentimental evocation of peasant life, a hymn to the tenacity of love and a Brechtian fable about the world's unfairness.' Of the Théâtre de Complicité, Berger wrote: 'Lucie Cabrol was a smuggler. Théâtre de Complicité are also smugglers in that they ignore frontiers and cross them without official papers . . . Thus this theatre smuggles the public in to places which are normally considered closed. And they smuggle out of those distant places the daily routines and the triumph and the pain of being alive . . . Contraband nevertheless. Contraband because it's about what is habitually marginalized, dismissed, belittled, made voiceless. Maybe the essential contraband today is hope. Hope which is inseparable from life, like the violent theatre these gentle artists make.'

4 Showing Voice

1   *Play Me Something* 'only cost a couple of hundred quid to make', Berger
    once told me, with modest aid from the British Film Institute and
    Scottish Film Production Fund. The cast includes Scottish poet and
    folklorist-songwriter Hamish Henderson, who plays an eccentric TV
    electrician, a listener driving a horse and cart. In 1993 Berger and Neat
    embarked upon another film together, *Walk Me Home*, similarly set in
    the Outer Hebrides. The film was never completed; everything that
    could go wrong went wrong, Berger confessed to me: 'It was a balls up!'
    Jean Mohr, who was photographing the filming, provides testimony:
    'I eventually found a room were the team had gathered', Mohr said.
    'About fifteen of them. The place was thick with cigarette smoke, the
    faces inscrutable, the tension palpable . . . They seemed to be discussing
    essential themes and the decisions that needed to be taken about
    the rest of the shooting. It was written all over John's face that he was
    having a bad day; from time to time he stammered, tugging at his thick
    hair as if it might provide him with a solution' (see Jean Mohr, *At the
    Edge of the World*, London, 1999, p. 166).

2   The narrator of *Lilac and Flag* (1990), the third and final book of
    Berger's peasant saga, is an old woman who stayed in the village while
    others left. Year after year she has watched people disappear and never
    come back, year after year she has watched them disappear in the city
    and loose themselves in the city. In Berger's later 'novel' *To the Wedding*
    (1995), the narrator is an old blind Greek man, unseeing yet all-hearing,
    who sells little *tama* objects that can be recognized by touch. This old
    man has found the storyteller's muse: 'Voices, sounds, smells bring gifts
    to my eyes now', he says. 'I listen or I inhale and then I watch as in a
    dream.' When *To the Wedding* was brought to BBC Radio 3 in 1997 (by
    Berger and Simon McBurney's Théâtre de Complicité), a blind man
    as narrator posed certain structural difficulties. So instead Berger's
    storyteller miraculously became the Po, Italy's longest river!

3   The citation comes from *And Our Faces, My Heart, Brief as Photos*
    (London, 1984), p. 57. Interestingly, in *Imaginary Homelands* (London,
    1991), Salman Rushdie sympathetically confronts Berger. 'One can
    appreciate the compassion of Berger's vision', Rushdie says, 'and admire
    the brilliant originality of *A Seventh Man*, and still wish to start pushing

beyond such apparent despondency. To migrate is certainly to lose language and home, to be defined by others, to become invisible or, even worse, a target; it is to experience deep changes and wrenches in the soul. But the migrant is not simply transformed by his act; he also transforms his new world. Migrants may well become mutants, but it is out of such hybridization that newness can emerge' (p. 210).

5 Animal Humanism

1 In his essay 'Mother' Berger discusses his mother's vegetarianism. Later in life she ate meat; but on her deathbed Berger asked why had she been a vegetarian. 'Because I'm against killing. She would say no more.' 'In time', he reflects, hinting at his mother's influence, 'I chose to visit abattoirs in different cities of the world and to become something of an expert concerning the subject.' (Berger's essay is reprinted in *Keeping a Rendezvous*, London, 1992).

2 Berger's classic essay features as the mainstay of a handy new collection of his animal writings, entitled *Why Look at Animals?* (London, 2009).

3 In Robert Bresson's *Au Hasard Balthazar*, a 1960s film about an abused donkey called Balthazar, there's an especially haunting, Bergeresque scene involving the gaze of animals. Balthazar is employed as a circus act, as an entertaining donkey that does sums before an audience: he is asked to multiply a series of big numbers and duly stamps his hoof a certain number of times to signify the answer. When Balthazar first arrives at the circus he is dragged around the enclosures, around cages housing other animals. His eyes make contact with other eyes, amid long silent stares – lingering stares that seem to last forever. There's no animosity or pity between the helpless animals. First he is eyeballing a tiger, behind bars; then a polar bear, then a chimpanzee; then, the longest, and most moving, with an elephant, whose beady little eyes grip Balthazar's. We can almost see the latter's water for an instant, before he's dragged away. Each party seems cognizant of their respective fate; each party is communicating in a secret language: it's us humans, they all silently concur, who are the real circus acts; it's us who are really behind bars, in captivity.

4 He-goat and donkey can be glimpsed in *Par la fenêtre*, a catalogue to an

exhibition of Berger's drawings and his son Yves' paintings that took place in Germany in 2009, at Issing's Galerie Josephski-Neukum.

5 Berger wrote and sent these lines – lines that would make it into *King: A Street Story* (London, 1999) – on black paper next to his panting dog, to the artist and filmmaker John Christie. For several years, between 1997 and 1999, the two Johns exchanged ideas, thoughts, images and sometimes small, home-baked books about *colours*, about their tones and tendencies, about their meanings and memories. The fascinating kaleidoscope correspondence has been put together by Eulàlia Bosch in a work called *I Send You this Cadmium Red: A Correspondence between John Berger and John Christie* (Barcelona, n.d.).

6 Berger, 'Opening a Gate', *The Shape of a Pocket* (London, 2001), p. 5.

7 Berger, *King: A Street Story*, p. 227. In May 2005 a 'scratch performance' of Berger's dog story was staged in an East London squat, put on by Cardboard Citizens. 'They were mad to try . . .', an ad for the performance said. 'They were mad to try to lead you to where they live.'

8 This is a 'Joycean' paraphrase of a Berger line first uttered in 'Dix dépêches sur le sens du lieu', *Le monde diplomatique*, August 2005. 'Ten Dispatches about Place' is reprinted in English in *Hold Everything Dear: Dispatches on Survival and Resistance* (London, 2007).

6 Amongst Other Things a Marxist

1 There are other similarities with *Capital*. Like Marx's great opus, *A Seventh Man* never really sold well either. On 29 August 1975, in a personal letter to Mike Dibb, Berger wrote: 'The reviews [of *A Seventh Man*] were not very bright. The book works, I know. And the price is fantastic. Yet I fear it's not selling. Only 3,000 in the first month, which is nothing.' Later in the autumn, Berger told the same Dibb: '*A Seventh Man* is doing disastrously. In three months, Penguin have sold less than 2,000 copies! It makes no financial difference to Jean [Mohr] and myself – since Penguin are *charging us* nearly £500 for extra printers' bills. (Perfectionism is expensive.) And, along with our advance, this means that if it sold 30,000 copies we wouldn't get a penny. It's not that. It's that the book should be read. The people who have responded very intensely to it are migrants: Turks, West Indians, Portuguese, etc.

One day the book will become a little "classic" but by then its *force* will have become polite.'

2 The *here* in *A Fortunate Man*, its precise location, is never mentioned in Berger's text; typically, Berger's style is to show rather than tell. John Sassall (aka John Eskell) had his practice in the Forest of Dean, in the west Gloucestershire village of St Briavels, where he healed the town folk until his retirement in April 1982.

3 The French translation of *A Fortunate Man* puts another spin on Sassall, shifting the emphasis from who he is to what he does. His activity is somehow *un métier idéal*, an ideal trade or craft, an ideal job. The semantic shift makes it perhaps tally more with young Marx's conception of 'total man', which stresses the importance of free conscious *activity* in releasing 'the practical energies of man'. So, in *doing* we can *be*.

4 Eskell (Sassall), who died at the age of 63 on 16 August 1982, had been dogged by poor health for over a decade before he ended his own life. His wife's death, in 1981, also hastened his own. The *British Medical Journal* ran Eskell's obituary on 9 October 1982. Berger's 'The Secretary of Death', meanwhile, first appeared in *New Society*, 2 September 1982.

5 Some of Berger and Neizvestny's correspondence – drawings, postcards and letters, at first in French, later in English – are amongst Berger's archives at the British Library. One missing piece of correspondence is a letter Neizvestny apparently wrote to Berger not long ago, admitting that the latter may have been right about America being the wrong place for Neizvestny, that he felt isolated there despite the evident material trappings he had accrued.

6 *Art and Revolution* makes no reference to *Strange Births*. Berger only discovered the series of drawings later in 1969, after visiting Neizvestny in Moscow, sailing by boat to Leningrad with a six-year-old Katya in tow. The drawings had no name then, and Neizvestny worked on them every night, on the sly, over many, many years. Berger says he smuggled each frame out and hid them under Katya's bunk on the return voyage. KGB agents followed Berger, searched his cabin, but they left Katya sleeping and thus *Strange Births* made it back to Geneva. Afterwards, they were reconstructed in a London studio and used for Vas' 'An Artist in Moscow' (Berger, conversation with the author, 9 November 2010).

7 Marcos' 'The Fourth World War Has Begun', first published in *Le monde*

diplomatique (September 1997, English edition), is available online at
http://mondediplo.com, accessed 20 July 2011.

8 Berger, *The Shape of a Pocket* (London, 2001), pp. 221–2.

9 Marcos, in Berger, *The Shape of a Pocket*, pp. 230–31.

10 Berger, 'Ten Dispatches About Place', *Hold Everything Dear: Dispatches on Survival and Resistance* (London, 2007), p. 125.

7 About Time and Space

1 Berger's preceding citation comes from *And Our Faces, My Heart, Brief as Photos* (p. 34), which partly inspired *About Time* (London, 1985). *About Time*, the book that accompanied the television series (edited by programme co-director Chris Rawlence), opens with Berger's essay 'Once upon a Time', the title of the first programme, the only one in which Berger actually appears. On *About Time*'s back cover, Berger wrote: 'through our different experiences and lives, we had come to the conclusion that the notions about time, which are embodied today in formal education, the current assumptions of news bulletins, political promises and moral sermons, are patently inadequate. What we wanted to do [in the television series] was to clear a space that could be given over to other, more intimate, less rhetorical and more far seeing intuitions and questions which cluster, for the most part unacknowledged, around everyone's experience of time, and then let these intuitions talk with science and history.'

2 *Here is Where We Meet* also became the rubric of a major Berger retrospective held in London in spring 2005. The season announced a celebration of 'culture, collaboration and commitment'. Throughout April and May Berger's films, documentaries and plays were shown and performed, and live interviews, readings and discussions were staged with Berger himself, alongside a host of friends and colleagues including Michael Ondaatje, Anne Michaels, Jean Mohr, Geoff Dyer, Mike Dibb, John Christie, Maggi Hambling, Nella Bielski and Simon McBurney. In the wonderful catalogue for the event, Berger is cited: 'I can't tell you what art does and how it does it, but I know that art has often judged the judges, pleaded revenge to the innocent and shown to the future what the past suffered . . . Art, when it functions like this,

becomes a meeting-place of the invisible, the irreducible, the enduring, guts and honour.'

3 Berger, *The Look of Things* (New York, 1974), p. 40.
4 This citation, and the ones which follow, are taken from Berger's short pamphlet *Meanwhile* (London, 2008). In an interview with the *New Statesman* (18 January 2010), Berger said that if somebody knew nothing about him, and wanted to know him a little, he would send them two books: *A Seventh Man* and *Meanwhile*. 'Prison', he added, 'it keeps coming up, doesn't it?'

8 Confronting Walls

1 Berger, 'A Moment in Ramallah', *London Review of Books*, 24 July 2003, p. 22.
2 'Wounded red' is, of course, one of the colours Berger exchanged with John Christie in their book *I Send You This Cadmium Red: A Correspondence between John Berger and John Christie* (Barcelona, n.d.).
3 Darwish, who'd had a history of heart problems, died in Houston, Texas, on 8 August 2008 at the age of 67. The cause of death was complications following heart surgery at the city's Hermann Memorial Hospital. Not long after the Bergers' pilgrimage, Darwish's grave, following a decision made by the Palestinian Authority, was fenced off; a glass pyramid has since been built over it and it is no longer possible to sit on the bare earth beside him.
4 Mahmoud Darwish, *Entretiens sur la poésie* (Arles, 2006), pp. 39–40.
5 Walter Benjamin, 'The Task of the Translator,' *Illuminations* (New York, 1968). It ought to be said that Berger was no stranger to translation. He'd worked with, and learned a lot from Anya Bostock, with whom he had translated Brecht and Aimé Césaire's *Return to My Native Land* from the original French. 'This is not a free adaptation of Césaire's work', Bostock and Berger wrote in their 'Translators' Note' to the Penguin 1969 first edition; 'neither, however, is it a completely literal translation', they added. 'The poem is important because of its thinking content. The thinking is both political and poetic. Politically it is a poem of revolutionary passion and irony. Poetically its images have a physical and often sexual resonance. It is always in respect to this double content

that we have sought and worked upon an English version.'

6   Berger, conversation with the author, 9 February 2011.

7   Mahmoud Darwish, *Mural*, trans. Rema Hammami and John Berger, (London, 2009), pp. 50–51.

8   In Mike Dibb's documentary *A Telling Eye*, Jean Mohr notes of his old friend and collaborator: 'what I appreciate most is how John goes up and down, and is very expressive; I'd be tempted to say like a woman sometimes, though it would be wrong because it doesn't belong only to women to be so expressive, so warm . . . But he's not afraid of his emotions, of expressing them openly. I've seen John crying when I haven't cried for forty years.'

9   Interview, *Weekend Financial Times*, 4–5 June 2011.

10 See Berger, *Le blaireau et le roi* [*The Badger and the King*] (Geneva, 2010), pp. 179–80.

11 The term is Gilles Deleuze's from *The Fold: Leibniz and the Baroque* (Minneapolis, MN, 1988). A fold, says Deleuze, announces that the inside is nothing more than a fold of the outside, and vice versa. Life is manifold; subjectivity unfolds; our bodies experience the folding of time; our best architecture creates intimate spaces that envelop one another, and us; caverns fold into other caverns, and so on. The imagery of folds (*les plis*) is used in Yves Berger's long poem, *Destinez-moi la Palestine* [*Make Palestine My Destiny*], consecrating his first West Bank sojourn: 'Folds of the sky: folds that are your source./ Terrace in the creases for uniting water and roots.'

12 Berger, *Keeping a Rendezvous* (London, 1992), p. 87.

9 Spinoza's Motorbike

1   Robert Pirsig, *Zen and the Art of Motorcycle Maintenance* (London, 1974), p. 12.

2   There's another 'coincidence' as well, and that's George Steiner, the influential critic who extolled the virtues of both books in the pages of *The New Yorker*, giving them each a lift within a year or so of one another, comparing *G.* to *The Man Without Qualities* (27 January 1973) and *Zen* to *Moby-Dick* (15 April 1974). The outsiderness of both books, Steiner said,

both authors' passion for big ideas, their courage in not disguising this passion, their fragmentary, patchwork approach that avoids pure narrative form, coupled with their affirmation of essentially *passive* heroes, unites Pirsig's and Berger's art. Both works, Steiner said, are works of high literature; both are books written for adults.

3   Berger lent me a wonderful handmade maquette of *Bento's Sketchbook*, his only copy, prior to its publication. So *Bento's Sketchbook* became a fascinating glimpse of *Berger's Sketchbook*, of his annotated prose, of his crossings-out, of his finger-smudged drawings. If Berger was trying to access Spinoza's workshop, as well as the mind behind those propositions and demonstrations, now I could enter Berger's own workshop, see the private gleam of his unpolished diamonds. What was evident was Berger's hesitancy about the title, which seems to have initially been conceived as *Good to Know You* (after Woody Guthrie's song). In one of a series of lengthy telephone conversations Berger told me that his reading of Spinoza had been greatly influenced by Gilles Deleuze's, whom Berger 'admires enormously'. He even gives his friends the double CD *à haute voix* of Deleuze's *Spinoza: immortalité et éternité*, recordings of the famed Spinoza class the late philosopher gave at the University of Paris VIII. 'What a teacher!' Berger said of Deleuze.

Select Bibliography

Books by John Berger

A Painter of Our Time (London: Secker & Warburg, 1958)

Permanent Red (London: Methuen & Co., 1960)

The Foot of Clive (London: Methuen & Co., 1962)

Corker's Freedom (London: Methuen & Co., 1964)

The Success and Failure of Picasso (Harmondsworth: Penguin, 1965)

A Fortunate Man, with Jean Mohr (Harmondsworth: Penguin, 1967)

Art and Revolution: Ernst Neizvestny And the Role of the Artist in the USSR (London: Weidenfeld & Nicolson, 1969)

The Moment of Cubism and Other Essays (London: Weidenfeld & Nicolson, 1969)

G. (London: Weidenfeld & Nicolson, 1972)

The Look of Things: Selected Essays and Articles (London: Weidenfeld & Nicolson, 1972)

Ways of Seeing, with Mike Dibb, Sven Blomberg, Chris Fox and Richard Hollis (New York: Penguin, 1972)

A Seventh Man, with Jean Mohr (Harmondsworth: Penguin, 1975)

About Looking (London: Writers & Readers Publishing Cooperative, 1980)

Another Way of Telling, with Jean Mohr (Cambridge: Granta, 1982)

Jonah Who Will be 25 in the Year 2000, with Alain Tanner (Berkeley, CA: North Atlantic Books, 1983)

And Our Faces, My Heart, Brief as Photos (London: Writers & Readers Publishing Cooperative, 1984)

The White Bird (London: Chatto & Windus, 1985)

A Question of Geography, with Nella Bielski (London: Faber & Faber, 1987)

Goya's Last Portrait, with Nella Bielski (London: Faber & Faber, 1989)

Into Their Labours: A Trilogy (London: Granta Books, 1992) (comprises *Pig Earth*, 1979, *Once in Europa*, 1989, and *Lilac and Flag*, 1990)

Keeping a Rendezvous (London: Granta Books, 1992)

Pages of the Wound (London: Bloomsbury, 1994)

To the Wedding (London: Bloomsbury, 1995)

Photocopies (London: Granta, 1996)

Titian: Nymph and Shepherd, with Katya Berger (London: Bloomsbury, 1996)

Isabelle: A Story in Shorts, with Nella Bielski (London: Arcadia Books, 1998)

At the Edge of the World, with Jean Mohr (London: Reaktion Books, 1999)

King: A Street Story (London: Bloomsbury, 1999)

I Send You This Cadmium Red: A Correspondence with John Christie, with John Christie and Eulàlia Bosch (Barcelona: Actar, 2001)

Selected Essays, Geoff Dyer, ed. (London: Bloomsbury, 2001)

The Shape of a Pocket (London: Bloomsbury, 2001)

Berger on Drawing (Aghabullogne, Co. Cork: Occasional Press, 2005)

Here is Where We Meet (London: Bloomsbury, 2005)

Hold Everything Dear: Dispatches on Survival and Resistance (London: Verso, 2007)

From A to X: A Story in Letters (London: Verso, 2008)

Meanwhile (London: Drawbridge Books, 2008)

From I to J, with Isabel Coixet (Barcelona: Actar, 2009)

Why Look at Animals? (London: Penguin, 2009)

Bento's Sketchbook (London: Verso, 2011)

Cataract, with Selçuk Demirel (London: Notting Hill Editions, 2011)

Railtracks, with Anne Michaels (London: Go Together Press, 2011)

Feature Films

La Salamandre, scenario with Alain Tanner (Filmograph SA, Switzerland, 1971)

Jonas qui aura 25 ans en l'an 2000, scenario with Alain Tanner (Action / Citel Films, Switzerland / France, 1974)

Le Milieu du monde, scenario with Alain Tanner (Action / Citel Films, Switzerland / France, 1974)

Play Me Something, directed by Timothy Neat (BFI, 1989)

Walk Me Home, directed by Timothy Neat (BFI, 1993)

TV Documentaries

BBC 'Monitor' series:
'Giacometti' (1962)
'Picasso' (1964)
'Release: de Stijl' (1965)
'Why Leger?' (1965)
'Le Facteur Cheval' (1966)
'An Artist from Moscow' (1969)

'La Ville à Chandigarh', with Alain Tanner (1966)
'A Fortunate Man' (1967)
'Ways of Seeing', with Mike Dibb (1972)
'Pig Earth', with Mike Dibb (1979)
'About Time: Once Upon a Time', with Mike Dibb (1980)
'Parting Shots from Animals', with Mike Dibb (1980)
'Germinal' (1983)
'Another Way of Telling', with John Christie (1989)
'A Telling Eye: The Work of John Berger', with Mike Dibb (1993)
'The Spectre of Hope', with Sebastião Salgado (2000)
'Art, Poetry and Particle Physics', with Ken McMullen (2005)

Translation

Bertolt Brecht, *Poems on the Theatre*, with Anya Bostock (Northwood, Middlesex: Scorpion Press, 1961)
Aimé Césaire, *Return to My Native Land*, with Anya Bostock (Harmondsworth: Penguin, 1969)
Nella Bielski, *Oranges for the Son of Alexander Levy*, with Lisa Appignanesi (London: Writers & Readers Publishing Cooperative, 1982)
Nella Bielski, *The Year is '42*, with Lisa Appignanesi (London: Bloomsbury, 2005)
Mahmoud Darwish, *Mural*, with Rema Hammami (London: Verso, 2009)

Books on Berger

Geoff Dyer, *Ways of Telling: The Work of John Berger* (London, 1986)
Nikos Papastergiadis, *Modernity as Exile: The Stranger in John Berger's Writing* (Manchester, 1993)

Further Reading

Walter Benjamin, 'The Work of Art in the Age of Mechanical Reproduction', in Benjamin, *Illuminations*, ed. Hannah Arendt (New York, 1969)
Ernst Fischer, *The Necessity of Art* (London, 2010)
Georg Lukács, *The Theory of the Novel* (Manchester, 1978)
Spinoza, Baruch, *Ethics*, ed. G.H.R. Parkinson (London, 1993)

Acknowledgements

Thank you, John, for your cooperation and support for this project, as well as for your inspiration over the years. Thank you, Mike Dibb (and Cheli Duran), for your hospitality during my London visits, and for your friendship and infectious enthusiasm. (Thanks, Mike, for letting me plunder your archives and pick your brains.) Thank you, too, Vivian at Reaktion, for commissioning the book and for your helpful comments on earlier drafts. And thank you, Corinna, for understanding how all my intellectual voyages somehow turn into strange voyages of self-discovery.

Photo Acknowledgements

The author and the publishers wish to thank the below sources of illustrative material and/or permission to reproduce it:

Mike Dibb Collection: pp. 39, 78, 79, 148, 149; Jean Mohr, Musée de l'Elysée, Lausanne: pp. 6, 10, 11, 13, 16, 21, 36, 72, 137, 141; Motorcycle International: pp. 191, 193; Maria Nadotti: p. 169.